P9-CMV-562

Writing and Selling Greeting Cards

OREGON

DEC 13 1984

STATE LIBRARY

Writing and Selling Greeting Cards

by

CARL GOELLER

DISCARD

❧

Publishers   THE WRITER, INC.   *Boston*

WITHDRAWN
FROM E.O.U. LIBRARY

Eastern Oregon University
1410 L. Avenue
La Grande, OR 97850

Copyright © 1980

by

CARL GOELLER

Library of Congress Cataloging in Publication Data

Goeller, Carl G.
  Writing and Selling Greeting Cards.

  1. Greeting cards industry—United States.
I. Title.
HD9839.G73U54   808'.025   79-25543
ISBN 0-87116-124-9

Printed in the United States of America

This one's for Kim

ACKNOWLEDGMENTS

Sincere thanks to the American Greetings Corporation and its president Irving Stone for the use of many of their sentiments and gags; to Hallmark Cards and Rust Craft Publishers, for the years of valuable experience gained there and for the use of sentiments and gags from their greeting card lines; for the advice and assistance of industry professionals Rowena Cox, Casey Beregi, Colleen Gutta, Jane McKinley, Kem Mahon, and Caroline Martlew; to Sue Kennedy and my wife, Kay Goeller, for their help in preparing the manuscript; and to my son, Ben, for helping to make the time available to me to write this book.

Contents

✑ CHAPTER 1
Where It All Began

THE HISTORY of the greeting card can be summed up in one word—change. In two words—constant change. In three words—predictable constant change.

Easily 80% of all written material turned down by editors is done so with comments like "that's old hat; we've seen it before!" "It might have sold 10 years ago, but not today!" or the especially damning, "I have a whole file full of that kind of thing!" Conversely, 80% of everything an editor accepts should strike him as something fresh, and possibly unusual enough to strike a spark in the marketplace. It stands to reason, then, the more you know about this market, the higher will be your acceptance rate.

The greeting card officially emerged in this country around 1840 with the first published Christmas card, but it didn't become a mass-produced item until shortly after the Civil War when the small printers who published cards couldn't keep up with the demand created by the war. Around 1870, Louis Prang, an enterprising Boston lithographer, began mass producing Valentines and Christmas cards using designs from his extensive selection of calendars and art prints. It was he who first began using printed messages on the cards. Up to that time, most cards were blank and the purchaser wrote in his or her own message, usually copied in elegant handwritten script from books of pre-written sentiments. A typical example:

> Prithee receive this unpretending card,
> Prithee believe it carries my warm regard.

Louis Prang introduced the sentiment-design tie-in, although he had to do some contriving at times to work in the season of his existing artwork. For example, the painting on one of his cards depicted sailors from a British frigate rowing towards shore. The message read:

> Onward through smooth waters
> May you gaily steer this Christmas!

The turn of the century brought the passing of Prang, and the coming of many new publishers into the field. During the period 1906 to 1919, all the major card companies we now know—American Greetings, Rust Craft, Norcross, Gibson, and Hallmark—came into being. With them came a deluge of new ideas, ranging from humor to timely greetings to novelty cards and later, the introduction of some good artists and famous writers. A World War I novelty card, for example, enclosed some Bull Durham tobacco and cigarette paper for the Yankee Doughboy and said:

> With this Birthday Card from me
> Comes the "makin's" as you see
> So shoot the Boche
>   and smoke the "Bull"
> Of Yank fighting, fill him full!

A humorous postcard of the era said frankly,

> I would if I could . . . but I can't . . .
> because I'm married now!

World War I and its subsequent separation of families and loved ones caused greeting cards sales to nearly quadruple, and by 1919, cards were an established part of American life. As such, they became more conversational in tone. Gone was the highly poetic message, including the "thees and thous" which had survived the turn of the century. The writing became more informal and timely. A typical verse of the 1920's read:

> Omigosh, I've fallen hard
> For no one else but you!
> Can't seem to get you off my mind
> No matter what I do!
> I like your smile, I like your style
> I like your snappy line
> And Omigosh, I wish you'd say
> You'll be my Valentine!

Cards reflected the topics of the time. Here's one:

> I may not be John Barrymore
> Or even Rudy Vallee
> But when it comes to lovin', Kid,
> Say . . . that's right down my alley!

The Great Depression had a great impact on the greeting card and its importance to Americans. Instead of collapsing, like many other businesses, this industry grew by leaps and bounds. Caught in a giant economic crunch, people substituted greeting cards for the gifts they couldn't afford on special occasions. For 5¢ or 10¢ they could let friends and loved ones know they cared . . . that thoughtfulness was alive and well, no matter what the economic climate. One early depression card showed a picture of Herbert Hoover and said,

> Prosperity is just around the corner . . .
> . . . and so is your Birthday. Hope it's happy!

Novelty cards, printed on paper towels, wallpaper, paper bags, and other cheap substances, kidded about hard times . . . and afforded a struggling nation some much needed laughter.

World War II ended the depression and catapulted the greeting card business into a major American industry. Cards for special people and occasions flourished, became available for soldiers, sailors, Marines, WACs, as well as every conceivable relative and other relationship. There were hundreds of cards available for the servicemen to send back home to family and sweethearts, initiating men to the habit of sending cards . . . something that had been "women's work" till then. An example:

> A Hello from your soldier boy!
> I've already been promoted . . . cross my heart, it's true
> . . . I'm one of their MAJOR problems
> and a GENERAL nuisance, too!

By war's end, greeting cards were as much a part of the American way of life as apple pie, hot dogs and filling stations.

Periods of national change and crisis continued to play an important role in the development of greeting cards. By the middle 1950's, colleges were flooded with veterans on the GI Bill. They seriously wanted an education, they were older, more sophisticated and more cynical than the traditional student and they did not like the conventional greeting cards on the market. So, in 1954 the studio card was born to meet the demands, needs and interests of this anti-establishment generation.

Studio cards were written and designed outside of the industry, by small maverick companies, and broke all the rules. Instead of nice sentiments, these cards said such things as "Drop Dead!" and "You want to lose ten ugly pounds? Cut off your head!" The art was contemporary—and outrageous. At first, major card companies thought they'd "ignore studio cards . . . they're just a fad and will quickly pass," but, young people loved them.

The major card publishers soon realized studios wouldn't go away, so they jumped into the market with slick, well-written, well-designed and market-tested cards which restored some of the "rules." The out-and-out slams became left-handed compliments, such as:

> Human beings I hate . . .
> . . . you I like!

Studio cards introduced risqué humor to the heretofore "pure" product. Some were borderline pornographic, but most relied on innuendo and double meaning. Some were as bold as:

> Candy is dandy . . .
> . . . but sex won't rot your teeth!

but others took the milder approach:

> Valentine, I'll give you my heart . . .
> . . . but you'll have to fight for the rest!

Throughout the early trial-and-error period of studio cards, one thing held true—the best sellers were those which included a me-to-you message, and the poor sellers were invariably those which did not. The more universal in appeal they were, the better they sold. A prime example is this classic:

> Fear not, some day your ship will
> come in . . .
> . . . and you'll be at the railroad station

The 1960's saw card customers buying more and more cards, which led to the introduction of "informal" cards—low-priced, with simple designs, brief sentiments, and somewhat "all purpose" sending situations. They were cute, rather than funny, and outsold traditional and studio cards by as much as three to one with casual messages like these:

> Just dropping by . . . to say HI!
>
> Just li'l ol' me . . . askin' how ya be?
>
> I only think of you twice a day . . .
> A.M. and P.M.

Girls could buy dozens and send one a day to their sweethearts away in the service. Friends could use them to keep in touch. They had universal appeal. As more men went overseas to Vietnam, the demand grew for cards that could be sent daily, and the "all purpose cards" began popping up in all lines—conventional, cute, humorous, and studio. And the card companies began introducing complete lines of no-occasion cards which they called Promotions. The sentiments grew warmer . . . often poignant:

> You made me what I am today . . .
>   Lonesome
> What's with you?
>   Wish it was me!
> I'd love to have your hand in mine right now . . .
>   . . . 'cause that'd mean the rest of you
>   wasn't too far away!

The beginning of the 1970's produced a new breed of young people—serious, socially conscious, and openly emotional. The turbulent, often violent sixties, seemed, paradoxically, to result in an emotional need for gentleness, tenderness, and sharing. It was during this *Love Story* era that the Soft Touch card was born. Soft Touch combined an almost poetic expression of deep emotions and romantic photographic designs for a tell-it-like-it-is realism. Buyers, mostly young people, loved them. Typical messages ran from direct expressions of love:

> Simply . . . sincerely . . . and deeply . . .
>   I love you
> It seems I couldn't love you more . . .
>   . . . but every day I do

to wistful expressions such as:

> somewhere . . . somehow . . . someway . . .
>   . . . someday

and unbridled optimism:

> I still believe in tomorrow

By the early 1970's, Soft Touch cards were being written for people of all ages, not just young people, money was reasonably plentiful, and the public was showing an interest in buying something a bit more expensive and permanent for its greetings. The industry responded with a wide line of what they called "greeting items." Basically, they were greetings in three dimensions. They ranged from beautiful ceramic collectors' plates—for example, this classic with American Greetings' trademarked old-fashioned little girl called "Holly Hobbie":

The time to be happy is now

—to funny figurines with statements like:

How much do I love you?
THIS MUCH!

to the extremely popular booklets called *Sunbeams*, which were often a 24-page collection of greetings strung together in story style. Studio cards became available at $1.00, $2.00 and $5.00 . . . and selling as fast as they hit the store. One $5.00 classic showed an enormous hippo and a tiny bird with the message:

I wuv you!

Once the traditional price barrier was broken, the major card companies enlarged their offerings to include permanent selections of calendars, posters, buttons, postcards, novelty stationery, ceramic and other 3-D merchandise. This greatly enlarged their need for good writing and fresh, new ideas.

The late 1970's witnessed an upsurge in special caption cards—cards for dieters, non-smokers, plant lovers, cards for dogs and cats to send and receive . . . even divorce cards such as this one:

> Your Divorce is a time for a fresh start,
> a new beginning . . .
> . . . and a new set of towels marked MINE

The industry began promoting heretofore non-existent holidays such as Secretary's Day and Grandparents Day. It also introduced topical cards on a regular basis, covering current events such as the energy crisis, the disco craze, oil spills, recession, inflation, politics, and current expressions taken from popular TV shows and commercials. Cards of the early 1980's reflect a cautious optimism. Typical spokesman of this philosophy is Ziggy, the lovable-loser, a syndicated cartoon character, who in one moment will say:

> Why worry about tomorrow . . .
> . . . we may not make it through today

and in the next:

> Thought for the day: As you go through the great
> shower bath of life, . . .
> . . . try not to slip on the soap!

then he will finally melt you with:

> Did you know I was put on this earth
> to bring joy and sunshine into your life?
> How am I doin' so far?

The history of this industry shows its continuous response to the times. Most of the major changes in greeting cards have been as a result of social and economic crises, which brought about changes in lifestyles, attitudes, relationships, and even senses of humor. There is a constant action-reaction movement by the card companies to the times and to competition.

The times may force new design styles, new language, new humor, and even new directions as a result of pressures from cost, production capabilities, etc. Did you know, for example, that studio cards started out to be the same size and shape as regular cards—square? The small company that began the whole thing was forced into a reprint situation due to skyrocketing sales, but had no square envelopes to fit the merchandise. So they obtained a large quantity of business-size envelopes—the long, slender type—and redesigned the cards to fit the envelope. The new size and shape was immediately termed "sophisticated" and an entire industry followed a lead with tall, slim cards.

Competition accounts for much activity and change. A new concept by one company will stimulate dozens of efforts by competitors to close the sudden gap in sales. American Greetings, for example, introduced Soft Touch cards in the spring of 1970. By the following spring, every card company in the industry had soft touch type cards.

What can you do about all this? As you write for the greeting card market, you must be alert to the changing times and the ups and downs they bring. Here are some suggestions:

1. *Keep your ideas timely.* Update your vocabulary regularly. Remember, our English language is changing faster today than at any time in its history. This doesn't mean that you should use the "hip" terms or "rock" slang—that changes too fast, almost to the point of confusion. Rather, use "in-words" and expressions that look as though they will be around awhile—for example, "Hang in there!" Purge your material of the "out" words as they take on new meanings or simply become archaic. For example, this bestseller of the 1950's:

> Be lighthearted, be gay
> Have a wonderful day!

The word "gay" is out now because of its present attachment to the homosexual community.

2. *Be alert to "action" as it happens.* That way you can be on hand with some good, salable re-action. For example, as soon as the Soft Touch card was established as a strong "action" force, an enterprising writer came up with the idea of using straight Soft Touch copy on the cover of the card, then switching to humor inside, for a Soft Touch spoof. Example:

> You are gone, yet I still feel your warmth encircling my body as your arms once did . . . I can still feel your lips against mine . . . and I remember the words we spoke then . . .
>
> mmmphmm . . . ffmmmph . . mmmmmmmm!

3. *Keep up with trends in the marketplace.* Don't just be a re-action writer—be an *action* writer. Be there first with ideas that meet the shifting markets. Soft Touch responded to a gigantic youth market in 1970. What ideas will *you* have for the late 1980's when the majority of the population is over 55?

4. *Don't judge the marketplace by yourself.* You may be a typical greeting card customer . . . but chances are, you're *not.* And it is important that you weed out your own preferences and prejudices, and concentrate on today's (and tomorrow's) market. No matter how much you like the "good old days" and the cards that represented them, they will never be back. Nor will the cards of the future be built completely around your taste. Be objective. Watch, listen, learn . . . then write. You'll be surprised at how good your writing will be.

The history ahead of us will be fascinating to watch and fun to be part of. For the observant, alert card writer, it can be profitable, too.

CHAPTER 2

What Is a Greeting Card?

IT's NOT easy, this business of putting other people's feelings on paper. The greeting card companies know this, and that's why they're willing to pay you, and pay you well, for expressing emotions in a few words.

The greeting card business gobbles up ideas, designs and sentiments at a rate of well over one hundred thousand a year and prints more than ten million greeting cards every single day of the year. To keep up with this demand, the larger companies employ full-time staff writers to provide much of their material. But throughout the industry, there are fewer than one hundred of these professionals, and no matter how good or how prolific they are, they cannot meet *all* the demands for ideas. Some of the material must come from free lancers.

Before you start to write a greeting card it is important that you know what *is* a greeting card.

A greeting card is just that . . . a card that greets! It's a piece of paper with some artwork (usually pretty) and a few

15

words (usually friendly) to help people communicate with one another. If everybody had plenty of time, were articulate in conversation, or had a way with the written word, there would be no need for greeting cards. People could handle all their communications themselves. But it doesn't happen that way. People are busier than they've ever been. Many are as reluctant to sit down and write a letter or pick up the phone and talk to a fellow human being as they might be to make a visit to the dentist or tax auditor. Most people feel themselves lacking in creative talent and readily admit they cannot draw a design or write a verse. And so they pay to have the job done for them. They buy a greeting card.

A greeting card is a substitute letter, visit or phone call. But it's a very special substitute because it has to conduct some very *personal* business. It has the job of saying "I love you," "I care about you," "I share your happiness," "I share your sorrow," "I'm proud of you," "I'm ashamed of myself," "I miss you very much," "I wish you much happiness," "You're an important part of my life," "Here is something special for you," "Come on over and share some fun with me," "I'm sexually attracted to you," "I want you to laugh," "I feel like crying," "Thank you . . . for so much," "I think about you often," "You're a very special person," "I hope you are feeling better," "I hope you will recover," and so on.

You would be careful about entrusting someone else to express those thoughts and emotions for you; so is the greeting card customer. She is willing to delegate the job to a greeting card, but she is extremely particular about *which* card she will select to handle the job.

And that's where *you* come in. As a writer of greeting cards, you must be able to say *what* the card customers—the majority of whom are women—want to say, the way they want to say it.

A greeting card is a message. The *art* on a card has the responsibility of attracting a customer to that card, but the *message* is what will cause her to buy—or not buy—the card.

A greeting card is a transmitter, a conveyor, a communicator of thoughts and emotions between people. It is a personal expression of feelings from person to person, a *me-to-you message*.

A *me*-to you message. "Me"—the sender with something to say. She has thoughts and feelings she wants to express to another person. A writer steps into the sender's thoughts and speaks *for* her, finding the right words, putting them into the best form.

A me-to-*you* message. "You"—the magic word that gets attention faster than any other; salesmen, public speakers, politicians, advertisers all know that YOU means everything. This is true for card writers, also. YOU is the *first word* to consider using.

The simplest and most obvious me-to-you message is the expression "I love you." We all know it works and so we use it often. You wouldn't dream of replacing it with "Somebody loves someone" . . . and expect the same results. It's surprising, however, to see how many writers will submit something like this:

> Each day is a wonderful new adventure
> for two people in love.

The thought is universal, and warm, but this is only a statement, not a me-to-you message. How much more impact it carries when expressed like this:

> I love you . . . more than yesterday,
> less than tomorrow.

or when given a humorous touch like this:

> I love you more and more each day!
> Gosh, I can hardly wait till tomorrow!

Note the difference directness makes. Nobody could possibly write a *letter* without using "you"—and no one should write a *card* without using it, either.

Of course, you can *imply* personal pronouns in your sentiments without actually using the words "you" or "me." In a sympathy message, for example, you might say:

> May it help to know that
> others understand and care.

What you are actually saying is:

> I am hoping you are comforted in your time of sorrow by knowing that people who care about you—and that includes me—understand that you are saddened and grieved and that your sorrow and loss affect us, too.

In ten words you have implied all this, yet said it in a warm, natural, concise way. And it still sounds conversational, as letters always do and greeting cards always should.

A me-to-you *message*. "Message"—what the sender says; the thoughts and feelings she wants to express. The message is the reason for sending the card, and the reasons may be many: 1. *Important events*—birthday, anniversary, birth, promotion, and seasonal occasions (Christmas, etc.). 2. *Serious circumstances*—death, illness, personal tragedy or change in a person's life. 3. *Emotional situations*—parting, gratitude, loneliness, love, friendship, family ties.

A greeting card is a complete communications package. A common problem of would-be card writers (and artists) is a misconception that a greeting card can be one-dimensional, that it can be a complete, salable idea if any *one* of the components is present. It doesn't work that way. A greeting card is *not* just a piece of art. It is not just a cartoon, joke, riddle, pun, story, poem, rhyme, or unique design. No one of these things by itself makes a good card. Each element may accompany the me-to-you message and make it more appealing, but, without it there is no card, because no individual card component can carry thoughts or emotions from one person to another.

A greeting card should have universal appeal. In the card business, this is called *sendability*, and it's linked hand in hand with salability. It means that each greeting card a publisher makes must appeal to literally tens of thousands of purchasers. A single 40¢ birthday card, for example, published by a major manufacturer, may sell as many as a half million copies. When you realize that each card you write must fit the sending needs of hundreds of thousands of people, you can see how important it is to make your writing universal—and to omit any unnecessary limitations.

On the surface, this may look like an impossible task. We've already described a greeting card as one of the most personal products on the market, one that must therefore be carefully tailored to a buyer's individual needs. Every person who sends a card should feel it expresses her own feelings and fits her sending needs. She should feel that it was written just for her to send to the specific recipient she has in mind at that time. And yet we have to multiply this card buyer by several hundred thousand. Consequently, you must aim your writing at the universal aspects in life and avoid the specifics.

Let's start with the basics of *sendability*. The occasion for which a card is made is in itself a limitation. Once you say birthday on a card, for example, you can no longer use it for get-well, anniversary, Christmas, etc. If you add the relationship of the recipient—Dad, for instance—you've added another limitation. If you include the pronoun "I," only one person can send the card, still another limitation. Most of these are acceptable; there are millions of dads having birthdays, and millions of sons and daughters sending them cards. But when you go beyond those limitations, there is a danger of so narrowing the market that only a relatively small segment of buyers can send the card. Take this hypothetical example:

> To my tall, blonde, handsome Dad . . .
> . . . with a loving wish for every hair
> on your moustache.

Those people with dads who are short, not so handsome, have hair of other colors (or none) and are clean shaven, can't buy the card . . . no matter how much they might like the design. Here's a non-fictional example:

> I'm sitting here feeling
> ever-so-blue . . .
> Just rocking and knitting
> and thinking of you.

It's sendable by one person (probably female) who likes old-fashioned furniture and knits. Also, there is a light, somewhat cute ring to the words that make it sound feminine.

There are all kinds of hidden limitations to avoid: an accident card that jokes about "a tough break" can be sent only to people who break bones (there are lots of other kinds of accidents); a wedding congratulations card that implies the sender knows both the bride and groom well (usually the sender knows only one of the two well); a son card with "we" in it (such cards are often sent by only one parent); a wedding congratulations card with "I" in it (such cards are often sent by a couple); a daughter card with "we" in it (must be sent by both parents); a sister card that indicates it has to be *sent* by a sister (you lose all sales to brothers; it should be sendable by either); or a goodbye card with "I" in it (often sent by groups of people); or a St. Patrick's Day card that is made to be sent *by* someone who is Irish *to* someone who is Irish (many are from non-Irish or to non-Irish); a husband birthday card that says, "I'm sending you this" (most wives probably prefer to hand the cards to their husbands). The list is long—and important. You should give the matter of sendability considerable attention. These limitations can sneak up on you!

There *are* cards that are purposefully limited in sendability: boy baby congratulations, Father's Day from son, woman-to-woman birthday, illness cards to a permanent invalid, etc. But unless you're trying to make it specific and limited, work hard to make sure it *isn't*. Sendability means sales!

The best way to test the sendability of each card you write is to ask yourself, "Who would send this, and to whom?" If your answer indicated a limited market, take it back to the typewriter and see what you can do to make it more sendable.

Look at this one, for example:

> Happy Birthday to a gal who's 36-26-36 . . .
> . . . from a guy who's 20-20

Pierce Library
Eastern Oregon University
1410 L Avenue
La Grande, OR 97850

Few women fit these or any other specific measurements, which is its first limitation. Then, this card must be sent from a man to a woman, and, as written, it sounds as though he's an admirer, but not yet a fiancé or husband. Why not take the basic idea—that the recipient is an attractive, desirable woman, and the sender appreciates the fact—and put into an established sending situation—husband to wife. Instead of listing her measurements, simply imply that she's attractive, especially to him. Now we can say:

> Happy Birthday to my Wife,
>   the gal who's got that same old attraction
>   . . . from the guy who's still got that
>   same old reaction!!

Now another limiting idea:

> If you ever need me . . .
>   . . . look me up in the yellow pages under AVAILABLE

Whom would you send this to—for what are you available? But the Yellow Pages idea is clever. Let's try it on a Missing You card:

> I'm easy to find these days . . . just look me up
>   in the Yellow Pages . . .
>   . . . under LONELY
> I MISS YOU!

Sometimes changing a single word can convert a limited card into a more sendable one. For example, a card FOR my FAVORITE AUNT can be sent to only one of your aunts (most people have several), but a card TO a FAVORITE AUNT can go to nearly any aunt.

One final answer to "What is a greeting card?" *It is a commercial product.* Greeting card companies are in the business to make money. Most of them, especially the major publishers, are large, sophisticated corporations that spend sizable sums to research their market, evaluate the sales of their product. They have learned a great deal about the people who buy greeting cards—what they like, and often as important, what they dislike.

This answers the question "What is a greeting card?" for the buyer. But "What is a greeting card?" to a writer? The definition needs some enlarging; in the expanding, some greeting card terms need defining.

In the card industry, "sentiment" or "message" refers to the written material that conveys the idea. A sentiment may be written in prose (conversational thoughts expressed *without* rhyme or meter) or in verse (conversational thoughts expressed *with* the aid of rhyme and meter).

With these definitions, you'll be better able to deal with the three aspects of developing and writing cards: the OPENING, the DEVELOPMENT, and the CLOSING.

THE OPENING

The *opening* can take several forms. It might be a fresh idea, a piece of art, or some strong lead-in copy, or it *could* be all three. The purpose of the opening is to *attract.* You want to get the customer's attention, to indicate first of all that the card fits the purpose or occasion she has in mind (birthday, get well, anniversary, or whatever). You want to let the customer know at once that here is a card that suits her taste and/or that of the recipient (usually the art will accomplish this), and you want to give her some indication as to what she can expect inside the card.

Start with a good, strong idea. An idea is the starting point, the foundation for all cards. Every greeting card, from the smallest and least expensive, to the most elaborate, high-priced one, begins with an idea. All the skill with words, techniques, and tricks of the card business mean nothing unless there's a good idea to use them on. And if you can pack a fresh, sendable idea into every card you write, whether it's conventional, Soft Touch, studio, humorous, or juvenile, you will make a sale. Grinding out routine, tired sentiments that are merely words strung together will simply waste your time—and the editors'!

How can you recognize a good idea? The same way you can tell an interesting conversationalist from a bore! A good conversationalist has something different, stimulating, interesting, or amusing to say. A bore talks on and on without saying anything. It's the same with cards, and editors who read through mountains of written material have no trouble spotting the gems—they say something!

Finding an idea, however, is the hardest part of writing a card. Where do you look? *Everywhere!* In conversations, memories, books, magazines, observations of human nature and behavior, newspapers, movies, music, an overheard remark, a joke, a sermon, an ad. Wherever you hear and see thoughts and words, you can find an idea. And you should *write it down* as soon as it occurs to you so that it doesn't get away from you. Lost ideas are lost dollars.

Just about anything may yield a greeting card idea. One writer, for example, began toying with the movie industry's rating code and came up with this winner:

> This birthday card for you has been rated X . . .
>> . . . because you're Xtra Special!

That led to another:

> This anniversary card is rated GP . . .
>> . . . because it's for the world's Greatest Parents!

Another writer who had been facing an unresponsive typewriter all morning turned his gaze to a half empty bag of pistachio nuts on his desk, and came up with this gem:

> You know, Dad, having a kid like me
> is a lot like eating pistachios . . .
>> . . . you have to do a lot of shelling out
>> just for one little nut!

A writer was pondering an editor's "needs list" and began toying with the word "need." It began to take on special meaning, and applying it to the love relationship, she wrote a good-selling sweetheart message:

> I need you . . .
>> . . . I've never needed anyone so much!

That served as a springboard to another:

> You . . .
>> . . . are all I need.

Inanimate objects often serve as idea stimulators. One writer came up with this classic after a visit to her grandmother's quaint, old-fashioned living room:

> Your years are like rose petals
> Placed in a jar
> The more you have, Grandma,
> The sweeter you are.

Notice the effective *beginning* on these examples. Provocative words like these are the first thing the card customer sees!

> Rated X   Rated PG   Eating pistachios
> Years are like rose petals

or "magic" words like

> "you"   "I need you"

DEVELOPMENT

The development of your message is extremely important. This is where the "meat" is, and where your skill as a writer comes into play. You have attracted the reader's attention with a good opening—an idea. Now you must hold her interest while you deliver the rest of the message. The longer the sentiment, the harder this becomes. That's why it is essential to be conversational and concise. One way to achieve this is to keep offering the reader a new thought in each line right to the end. Here's an example:

> Thinking of you right this minute
> And every thought has wishes in it
> One for sunshine
> one for cheer
> one for things
> that you hold dear
> and one for joys that
> last all year.

This sentiment offers more vivid images to keep the reader interested:

> If you could count all the flowers in a field,
> raindrops in a puddle
> or stars in the sky . . .

> . . . you'd know how many times a day
> I think of you.

How much more interesting are these two sentiments than this collection of clichés:

> This brings a wish for happiness
> Because your birthday's here
> And an added wish for luck and health
> For each day through the year
> And because you're someone very nice,
> It's also come to say
> That all the very best in life
> Should always come your way.

It's the kind of thing editors pass over quickly because it's similar to so much else, and it's padded with the irritatingly familiar "It also comes to say." If you crown it with an idea, an organized plan that shows you've thought it through and have something definite to say, here's what you may come up with:

> For you—three special wishes
> Because your birthday's here—
> The first is for a day that's filled
> With happiness and cheer,
> The second wish is for a year
> That's perfect day by day,
> And the last is for the best in life
> To always come your way.

The sentiment won't set the industry on its ear, but it now has an idea and a logical "middle."

You will make more "hits" with your writing if you keep your messages brief and concise. Our 8-line "idea card," for instance, can be improved even more by converting it to prose. Look:

Three wishes for your birthday . . .
> a happy day
> a perfect year
> and life's best for you . . .
> always

Paring down your sentiments to get the directness you want may be downright painful. We all hate to give up something we've written. But remember, nobody's words are sacred, and you'll find that 90% of the time you can rewrite your first effort with better results. Rewriting is a natural and essential part of writing cards, and you can't be fainthearted about it; bravery increases with time, because you find you aren't *losing* by rewriting, you're gaining. And you can't expect editors to find time to rewrite your material for you; *they* expect *you* to do that before you submit it to them. The polished idea is worth the time and effort.

CLOSING

The closing of your card is what wraps it all up and makes the message complete. In the case of a conventional greeting, it may involve nothing more than a tagline. For example, if you write:

> Precious things
> Are all too few . . .
> Guess that's why
> There's just one you!

You have a good message, but what is the occasion for sending the card? That's where a HAPPY BIRTHDAY tagline comes in.

Sometimes the ending will be nothing more than an added "human" touch that makes the card seem more like conversation. Here's an example:

> So often when I'm alone even in a crowded place
> I think of you and need so much to reach out
> and tell you so. Today was like that.

In the case of humorous or studio cards, the ending is often the punchline, which should not only complete the message, but get the laugh. For example:

> A little birdie told me just what kind of
> birthday gift to give you . . .
> Cheap!

There are times when the ending may be actually longer than the body of the message, as in this card:

> You make my heart throb . . .
> . . . and my ear ring
> and my shower stall
> and my sun shine
> and my birch bark
> and my door jamb
> and my drum roll
> and my barn dance
> and my class ring
> and my teeter totter

Remember, every card must be a complete message, neatly packaged and ready for the consumer to sign her name to it.

Greeting cards for sale on racks and in shops today reflect costly research. One of the most important tasks the writer has in writing and selling greeting cards is to study the market. You must be your own research department. Become familiar with what's on the card racks today, and you will develop an intuition about what may appeal to the market tomorrow. But you must get a feel for what card customers are already buying before you can offer them something fresh and new.

Spend as much time as you can in card shops and card departments. Read, observe, analyze, compare, evaluate and learn. Never pass a rack or card shop without browsing through the sentiments and listening to what people say about them. Observe what customers pick up and buy, and what they put down and don't buy. The better acquainted you become with this complex product, the better your chances of writing greeting cards successfully.

꿍 CHAPTER 3

The Right Form for a Greeting Card Idea

ONCE you have an idea, you must find the best possible way to express it simply, concisely, and conversationally. What forms will you use? Rhyme and meter? Free verse? Prose?

For years and years rhymed and metered verse has been the "trademark" of greeting card messages. So much so, in fact, that people often refer to card messages as "verses" even though many are in prose. Rhyme is still used on a majority of conventional and juvenile greeting cards, even though today prose is not only accepted, but also preferred by certain editors.

RHYME

Rhyme has many advantages. It helps customers read the message more easily, especially in the case of long sentiments. It appeals to their sense of rhythm and often helps set the mood of the message. It makes the words seem somehow "special," perhaps because the sender feels rhyme and meter are creative "extras" they couldn't provide if they were writing the message themselves. Consider this card, for example:

> I looked and I looked
> And this card caught my eye
> And I thought, "That's the one!
> Just a card to say HI!"
> And you'll know that it's warm
> And sincere as can be
> Because it's for you . . .
> And it's coming from ME!

Now the customer might have written simply:

> Just a sincere "Hi!" for you . . . from me

The rhymed version conveys an exuberance and warmth that would be next to impossible in prose.

Rhyme has its disadvantages, too. Many times a writer uses it to achieve a desired "sound" but in the process ends up twisting the language out of shape, inverting normal word order and sacrificing grammar, good usage, and even good sense for the sake of rhyme and meter. For example:

> With this greeting comes a wish sincere
> For your merriest Christmas and happiest year

"Wish sincere" is simply not good conversational writing and was used only to set a rhyme with "year."

Rhyme is easy enough to recognize—we probably learned it first in nursery rhymes and have enjoyed it all of our lives in poetry, songs, advertisements, and all other kinds of writing where words are used. Rhyming is a wonderful tool in writing greeting cards. Essentially, rhyme is a similarity of sound, shared by two (or more) words, at the ends of verse lines. The rhyming syllables (or words, in the case of one-syllable words) have the same vowel sound, and the letters or sounds following this are identical. For example: *lot/got; knowing/showing.* The sounds ("l" and "g"; "kn" and "sh") preceding the rhyming syllable are different—the rhyming vowel sound ("o") and all following sounds ("t" and "-ing") are identical.

If you feel you need some help, consult a rhyming dictionary. There are a number of inexpensive ones on the market in both hardback and paperback. Resist the temptation of finding a cute rhyme and trying to write a verse around it. It can be done, of course, if you're experienced, but a good card is seldom written that way. Follow the order of a) me-to-you; b) idea; c) writing, and find verses that are appropriate to the sentiment.

Some writers are tempted to push around the words in a line, in an illogical order, to make them rhyme. This is called "forced rhyme," which describes it perfectly—the words rhyme only because you force an unnatural accent on a syllable, or reverse the order of the words for the purpose. For example:

> You're so delightful
> In every way!
> Sure hope you have
> A Happy Birthday.

"Way" and "birthday" make an irregular rhyme because the accent in the latter word falls naturally on "birth," not on "day." Such rhymes are amateurish. Avoid them!

Homonyms—words that are spelled differently but sound alike (*blue* and *blew*, *do* and *dew*, *for* and *four*, *one* and *won*) should not be used as rhymes in greeting cards. In order for two words to rhyme, they need unlike sounds preceding the rhyming syllable and the same number of syllables—*mother* and *another*, *dad*, and *glad* (in both sets, the accented parts are identical, but the parts before the accent are different). With all the rhymes available to you in the English language, you can find many alternatives to homonyms.

Other "sound-alike" words are "near rhymes," which is just what it says—two words that *nearly* (but don't quite) rhyme. Most card companies don't make a practice of using near rhymes, so you shouldn't feel free to use them at will. Now and then near rhymes do appear—*fine* rhymed with *time*, *wishes* rhymed with *kisses*. It takes skill to handle near rhymes and, again, it's best to use them when they intensify what you're saying to such a degree that you're willing to trade a true rhyme to convey that.

You might also try for freshness by using rhymes that extend for more than one syllable with the final syllable unaccented. For example: *yearly/dearly*, *going/showing*, *minute/in it*, and *visit/is it*. In the card industry, these are called "feminine" rhymes and are used primarily on cards intended for female recipients. On the whole, the industry prefers to use feminine rhymes on cards aimed at women and children, and occasionally on humorous cards.

Be careful, too, of what you rhyme with what. Take your speech pattern and regional accent into consideration. In some parts of the country, accents are unique and may jar the ears of those living in other areas. For example, in New England, *daughter* may rhyme with *quarter* and *doll* with *fall*. In the South, *moth* may rhyme with *north* and *born* with *dawn.* In some parts of the midwest, *can't* may rhyme with *paint* and *get* may rhyme with *hit.* Watch out for those rhymes which echo your particular accent and nobody else's; cards must sound right all over the country to sell.

You can add variety in your writing, too, by using a number of "rhyme schemes." A rhyme scheme is simply the arrangement of rhymes you're using. The most familiar is a four-line stanza called a quatrain, in which lines 2 and 4 rhyme. For example:

Hope your birthday's wonderful
In fact, your best so far   line 2
And that the more you have of them   rhymes with
The happier you are!   line 4

To make the often-used 8-line verse, put two of these four-line rhyme patterns together, rhyming lines 2 and 4 in each one. Another rhyme scheme you might use is the couplet, in which two lines rhyme. Again, as an example:

Just "Happy Birthday" from the heart   line 1 rhymes
'Cause that's where all good wishes start.   with line 2

You might write a four-line stanza of couplets in which lines 1 and 2 rhyme and lines 3 and 4 rhyme. For example:

THANK YOU . . .
For all the thoughtful things you do   line 1 rhymes
For sharing joys and problems, too,   with line 2
For warmth and kindness without end . . .   line 3 rhymes
For all it means to be your friend.   with line 4

There are many rhyme schemes, but unless you're quite advanced as a writer, and are looking for new worlds to conquer, you can do nicely with the ones above.

METER

Meter is the pattern of accented and unaccented syllables in words. When you tap your toe to music, you are keeping time to the accented beats: when you use meter in verse, you can "keep time" by writing a short (˘) mark for each unaccented beat and an accent (ˊ) for each accented beat. This combination of accented and unaccented beats is called a foot; put as many feet together as you need to make a line of verse and put them together in a pattern you choose. You'll get a smooth-flowing line that is easy to read. Meter is a very individual thing. You may think your verse is in regular meter, but an editor may stumble when reading it. Test your verse before submitting it. Does it flow naturally enough so a reader will not falter? A brief review of the most common metric patterns (the most common feet) may be of help.

Iambic meter is the most familiar form, because it's a pattern our spoken language falls into naturally. An iambic foot is one unaccented syllable followed by one accented syllable, shown like this: ˘ˊ to help you visualize what you hear. An example of iambic feet put together to make lines:

> To wish you Christmas joy and cheer—
> Enough to last you all the year!

Trochaic meter is an iambic foot turned backward; that is; ˊ˘ an accented syllable followed by an unaccented. Here are some lines of trochaic feet:

> All the time I think of you!
> Gosh, that's lots of fun to do!

Anapestic meter is two unaccented syllables followed by an accented syllable: ˘˘ˊ, and here are lines of anapestic feet:

Yes, your years are like rose petals pressed in a jar,
For the more that you have, Dear, the sweeter you are.

Dactylic meter is the opposite of anapestic; it has one accented syllable followed by two unaccented: and lines of dactylic meter are:

Hundreds of things could be said about you,
All of them compliments, all of them true . . .

There are many other kinds of metered feet, but these are the most commonly used in greeting card verse and the best to start with. In a four-line verse, there are usually four feet in lines one and three and three feet in lines two and four; to make an eight-line verse, just repeat the pattern. That isn't to say this is the *only* way it can be. Playing around with the meters and the number of feet in a line of verse can be fun and can add variety to your writing. Just remember that it's easy to let meter run away with you. Don't let it! It's a tool—a way of adding ease, speed, and pleasure to the reading of sentiments. But meter does not have to be *rigidly* observed—so long as the pattern breaks don't disturb the flow of thought. Just don't use padding to make the meter perfect. Padding is amateurish and can ruin good verse. A sentiment is padded when words are added *solely* to make a regular metric pattern. This is the kind of thing to avoid:

Because you're *so* perfect
In *just* every way,
Here's hoping you'll have
A *just* perfect day.

The italicized words were added as padding to make the meter perfect; unfortunately, this makes it far from perfect.

Padding is the lazy way. This sentiment, in order to be good, must be rewritten, and rewriting takes effort, so the lazy writer chooses to pad. Editors won't spend much time with this; it's a time-waster. It's better for a writer to have the right word with an irregular beat in the meter than to sacrifice the quality of the message just to keep the meter regular. Free verse is becoming prevalent in greeting cards and with some pleasing results. Free verse is verse free of rigid meter and rhyme, but it is not prose. It still has a flowing, easy way of leading the reader, and the thoughts it offers are still poetic. Here is a free verse from the poet Heine used as an inside left:

> The sea has its pearls,
> The heaven has its stars,
> But my heart, my heart,
> My heart has its love.

And another inside left is free verse with occasional, irregular rhyme:

> Softly, like a choir hums,
> Christmas comes . . .
> Silently, like falling snow,
> Quiet as a whispered prayer
> In the air . . .
> Soft as muted candle glow,
> It comes,
> Not with trumpet blare
> Or drums . . .

Free verse tends to be long, a bit poetic, and often doesn't lend itself to me-to-you messages—which is why you'll see it so often as an inside left. When used in a sentiment, it usually appears as a Soft Touch card or book.

Free verse and prose are similar in that both are unrhymed and unmetered. But they differ in content and style. Free verse is the intensified, emotional language of poetry.

PROSE

Prose is the language we speak in our daily conversations with one another, so it's only natural that it should be widely represented in greeting cards. When a greeting card editor asks for prose, however, he's looking for a rather *special* prose. It should contain all the ingredients of a good greeting card, but it must also have an element of creativity—an ability to express a message or idea with flair and freshness. An editor knows, for example, that anybody can write "Happy Anniversary to both of you and best wishes for the future." It's a solid message, but not enough to persuade a card customer to part with her money and purchase it. On the other hand, a message like this one is likely to make a sale:

> May a circle of love
>   unite your hearts
> as you celebrate the day
>   you TWO
>   became
>   ONE

Sometimes you can pep up your prose with the use of alliteration. This gives you the sound effects of rhyme combined with conversational prose. An example:

> Thanks so much
> You have the knack for being
>   extra nice

Repetition is another good device in pepping up your prose. Here's one way of using it:

> Some wonderfully warm
> and special wishes . . .
> for a wonderfully warm
> and special friend.

One of the most popular and best-selling types of prose employs the "rule of three"—using three of something in the message. The most common is wishing the recipient happiness "today . . . tomorrow . . . always," but it can be used in more elaborate wishes as well. Here's a classic:

> May you have
> The SPIRIT of Christmas
> which is PEACE;
> the GLADNESS of Christmas
> which is HOPE
> the HEART of Christmas
> which is LOVE.

Another approach using the "rule of three" is to take three words and build the rest of your message around them, as in this grandmother message:

> Warmer . . .
> brighter . . .
> nicer . . .
>
> That's how a grandmother like you
> makes the world!

Not all prose needs to be "tricky" to sell. Simple, direct messages using warm, well-chosen words are excellent ways to convey a message. This golden anniversary sentiment, for example, says it all:

> May you enjoy every golden hour
> of an anniversary filled with all
> the happiness you so richly deserve!

Don't neglect meter when you are writing prose. It is not the *same* as the regular patterns you use in writing verse, but if you choose your words carefully and think about their placement, they will have a natural rhythm that gives the message a special conversational touch. Notice the meter in this prose message:

> Grandma, you're a lot like spring . . .
> > sunny . . .
> > > cheery . . .
> > > > lovely . . .
> > > > > warm . . .
> > > > > and always welcome!

Don't restrict your sentiments to rhymed verse. Learn to work with prose, too. Practice writing prose regularly; try to convert some of your rhymed sentiments into prose. The better you become at prose writing, the more versatile you become as a greeting card writer.

TONE

Finally, you need to consider the tone of the sentiment and the language it uses as you develop your idea.

Tone in cards is like the tone of conversations: it varies in the degree of formality used to express the thoughts. You use one tone when talking to your sweetheart or spouse; another to address a friend; still another when you talk to your boss, mother, grandmother, neighbor, or children. These differences in tone must be reflected in cards as well as in conversations, and in writing sentiments you must make the tone appropriate for the relationship between the sender and recipient. Four basic tones are used in conventional cards:

A sentimental card is sincere and very intimate—not gushy or overdone or silly, but warm and personal. For example:

> For being so dear in every way,
>   I love you . . .
> For making me happy every day,
>   I love you . . .
> For doing the wonderful things you do,
> For making dream after dream come true,
> But most of all—for being YOU,
>   I love you!!!

A friendly card is also sincere and expresses personal feeling but in a less serious, more informal manner; affection is implied but not stated:

> Many happy returns
> Of your birthday to you!
> May all you are wishing
> Come happily true!
> May the year you're beginning
> Be the best one you've had,
> And all those that follow
> Be equally glad!

The casual card is lighthearted and breezy and is often coupled with a cute design. An example:

Let's the two of us pretend
I'm dropping by this minute
To bring this birthday greeting
With warmest wishes in it!

The dignified card is formal and more reserved; it is sincere and friendly but free of intimate wording or obvious emotion. For example:

Wishing you the very best
Of luck and health and cheer
For every new tomorrow
Throughout the coming year.

The difference in tone can be seen in these sentiments, most obviously because it is influenced by the idea, the meter used, the rhymes, and the choice of words. A staid, slower meter makes the card more serious, while the livelier, swifter-moving meter makes the card casual, informal.

Whatever the tone, the language used must be contemporary, acceptable, and in good taste. Avoid dated expressions—"pin a rose on you!" or "twenty-three skidoo." Avoid words that have changed in meaning—"gay" used so frequently on cards years ago is taboo now because the meaning has changed, and that's true of many other words. Avoid words that offend—"gal" and often "girl" aren't popular with feminists, and various other words used in the past have become taboo because they are offensive to many people. Obviously, the "fad" terms have to be discarded unless they're used in fast-produced, short-lived promotions—phrases like "right on" and "where it's at," for instance. Also avoid unfamiliar words whose meanings might not be generally known. And by all means use language that is appropriate for the occasion and the relationship between sender and receiver—nothing tasteless on a sympathy card; no slang phrases on cards to be sent from a child to older people. The one hard and fast "rule" for language on greeting cards is the same for language used anywhere—let it be appropriate for the situation and occasion.

You have the me-to-you message, the idea, a number of ways to combine them to create a card. When you finish, you can add an appropriate caption and a fitting tag line and then test the card for sendability. The result should be a good, well-written and salable greeting card.

CHAPTER 4

Conventional Cards

A CONVENTIONAL card is a serious sentiment written in a conversational manner; it is often in rhyme and meter but may be in prose. Usually it has a design and caption on the cover and the message with a tag line on the inside of the card.

Conventional cards are the bread-and-butter of the industry. They are traditional and sentimental, and that's why they are so well-loved by card senders. People are sentimental and they love tradition, and if that's a fault, it's one to be cherished. Buyers of conventional cards want their messages to be warm and sentimental, yet simple and direct enough to express their emotions, feelings and relationships.

Many poorly written conventional cards have appeared through the years—trite lines saying nothing, churned out to fill space inside a card; but rarely do you see those old "nothing" cards now. They are faded along with the artificial poetry and flowery prose admired in the Victorian age. There is no indication that any of them are missed.

45

Today's conventional cards must *say something*, carry a *me-to-you message*, and be *well-written*. That's no small order, as anyone who writes good conventional sentiments will tell you!

START WITH AN IDEA

Keeping a me-to-you message in mind, search for an idea for a conventional card. You might begin, for example, with a design-sentiment combination, such as comparing a tree-top ornament and a friend; or an ornament to a mother. Or you might compare the Christmas star to God's love:

> Just as the Star guided the wise men
> on that Christmas long ago,
> so may the brightness of God's love
> light your path to peace and happiness
> at Christmas and always.

Try a similar approach in a graduation sentiment, this time comparing graduation and a key:

> Warm congratulations!
> May your graduation be
> A wonderful occasion
> And a shining, golden key—
> The key to great achievements
> And all your dreams come true
> In the happy, golden future
> That's just ahead of you!

Staying with the comparison idea, you might develop the image of a wedding ring into this congratulations card:

> As the gold ring encircles your finger,
> so may love encircle your lives,
> keeping you happy and contented
> through long and wonderful years
> of sharing.

As you can see, one good idea can produce a number of cards. Be sure to jot down any ideas you get, even if you can't work them up at the time. Don't let them get away. Keep an "idea file" of clippings, jottings, ads, and anything else you find that has possibilities. They will be thought-starters you can use as aids in producing ideas for cards, and it helps to have something tangible. "Waiting for inspiration" is best left to ivory-tower poets and dreamers. For card writers, getting started is what counts, and anything that starts ideas flowing is valuable. One thing that leads to good ideas and then good cards is a list of the themes that appear again and again in conventional cards. A theme is a good starting point for an idea:

General wish—the whole sentiment dwells on wishing.

Love—the expression of love of any sort; usually combined with specific captions—sweetheart, mother, darling, husband, wife, etc.

Gratitude—gratitude or thanks in the sentiment may be combined with love or other themes.

Tribute—from a very casual compliment to the serious tribute, this theme expresses reasons for feeling grateful, proud, honored, lucky, etc.

Religious—ideas mentioning God, prayer, or other words that are expressly religious.

Semi-religious—the mention of blessing or prayer as part of a sentiment but no deep religious thoughts or direct reference to God or the Bible.

Don't Say It or Can't Say It—sentiment that indicates the difficulty of expressing feelings or the infrequent expression of feelings.

Descriptive—rather limiting sentiments because they describe the relationship between sender and recipient or the fine qualities of the recipient; usually seen in close-relationship captions like mother, wife, husband, etc.

Memories—a nostalgic sentiment that talks of the past and good things recalled or good times shared with the recipient.

Remembering—a milder form of the "Memories" theme that doesn't go into detail; used in more generally-sendable cards, while "Memories" is for the more specific, limited, closer relationships.

Thinking of you—a sentiment mentioning thoughts of the person receiving the card; may be anyone, friend or relative; in friendship, thoughts alone expressed; in other captions, thoughts plus a wish for the occasion; also used in permanent illness cards when "get well" cannot be stated.

Especially for you—a sentiment implying more than it says—a special closeness between sender and recipient; complimentary.

Missing You or Wish I Could See You—used in cards for friend or loved one when the two are parted; may be used with other themes in other captions.

There are variations and combinations of these themes. Thinking about them, associating your own memories and feelings with them, and letting your mind play with sending situations for the themes, can result in some good ideas. Also, this gives you already acceptable approaches to stating your ideas and aiming your cards at specific sending situations.

There are eight formulas to help you develop your ideas into salable sentiments for cards. They provide the framework upon which you can build sentiments. By practicing with these formulas—they lead you step by step as you develop ideas—you can form good writing habits for creating salable sentiments.

Formula 1: It's a fact

This formula is one of the basics in the industry. The sentiment begins with a statement of fact or belief. This may or may not be followed by an explanation of how this fact affects the relationship at hand. The sentiment is completed with a greeting or compliment. Some examples:

It's time for sending Christmas cards	Fact
And that means time to say	Explanation
You're someone who is thought of	Message
In a very special way!	

and a statement of belief:

This greeting is a special one	Belief
And here's the reason why	Explanation
It's meant for you, and after all	
You're quite a special guy!	Message

You will see "facts" and "beliefs" on hundreds of cards. Here are some examples of lead-in lines:

A house alone can't make a home . . .

Christmas is a time for friendships . . .

It's time for turkey and pumpkin pie . . .

Formula 2: Pose a problem

This is another frequently used formula; it often expresses the difficulty of saying what we feel. It begins by posing a problem (real or unreal). Next comes the solution; it may be exaggerated for complimentary effect or simply implied. A compliment results from the solution. Some examples:

Don't often get to mention this	Poses a problem
But today I'll tell you so	Offers a solution
You're very sweet and thoughtful	Message
And you're wonderful to know!	

"A very Happy Easter"	Problem
Doesn't seem enough to say	
To a brother who's so special	Compliment
And so fine in every way	
But maybe you will realize	Offers solution
As you read this message through	
It holds a lot more meaning	
When it's being said to you!	

Formula 3: It's very improbable

"If wishes were horses . . ." is always fascinating. The improbable appeals to everyone, including buyers of greeting cards. This formula begins with a statement of the improbable. It either becomes philosophical or discusses what would happen if the improbable happened. It ends with a compliment. For example:

If they counted birthday candles	Improbable
By the thoughtful things folks do,	
There'd be about a million	What would
On the birthday cake for you!	happen and
	compliment

If I could mail myself in person   Improbable
The way I'd like to do
I'd bring these wishes to your door   What would
To celebrate with you!   happen
   HAPPY BIRTHDAY   MANY MORE   and message

Formula 4: Flattery

Flattery is as popular in greeting cards as it is everywhere else. The sentiment begins with a compliment, the compliment continues, the end states the outcome of the compliment, which may be the sender's intention in sending the card. For example:

You're a wonderful person   Starts with compliment
Who's so nice to know   and continues with it
Because you make others happy
Wherever you go
No wonder you're wished   Compliment leads to
All the best things there are   a wish
And the loveliest birthday
That you've had so far!

        or

You're someone very special—   Compliment
You'd be hard to do without   Plus compliment
Because you're wonderful to be with Plus compliment
And you're nice to think about   then the message

Formula 5: Suppressed thoughts

Everyone has wishes and desires, whether stated or suppressed. This formula states those inner feelings—or tries to. First the desire, hope, or wish of the sender is stated (may include or lead to a compliment or a wish). The compliment follows, subdued or obvious. For example:

I'm wishing and wishing	The desire
with all of my might	
That your Christmas is perfect	The wish
from morning till night.	

or

I wish I could be half the friend	The desire plus
You always are to me	compliment
I wish I were the kind of help	Desire again
You're always glad to be . . .	and compliment
And at Christmas time I wish I could	again
In some small way repay	Leads to wish
A part of all the happiness	
You've given day by day—	
And if one wish were granted	Desire leads
This year, that wish would be	to wish and
That I could be just half the friend	compliment
You always are to me!	

Formula 6: Start with a Situation

First describe a situation, then follow it with the thought or message it prompts. At its simplest, the formula works like this:

I may be old-fashioned	Situation
But I don't care	
I love my wonderful mother—	Compliment
So there!	
HAPPY MOTHER'S DAY	

The situation may often relate to a season or card-sending situation such as this:

'Tis a fine Irish custom	Situation
I just couldn't miss	
To wish you good luck	Wish
On a grand day like this!	
HAPPY ST. PATRICK'S DAY	

It may also relate to some intimate knowledge of the recipient's personal life, as in this example:

We don't talk about it much	Sets up a situation
But, Dear, you know it's true—	
We've had the kind of happiness	
That comes to very few—	
A family we're proud of	Thoughts it prompts
A home that we hold dear,	
And a love that keeps on growing	Compliment
With every passing year.	

The situations which can be used with this formula are endless, especially in seasonal cards. For practice, try this formula using old stand-bys like these:

When it's time to greet another year   (New Year)
As spring flowers grace the earth once more   (Easter)
When leaves turn red and golden   (Thanksgiving)

Formula 7: Make a wish!

Up to this point, the formulas have used different methods of leading up to a wish or compliment. In this formula, you begin with your greeting, either clearly stated or disguised, then continue with a wish, and end with another wish or compliment. Here's a basic example:

Wishing you sunshine, Love and laughter	Begins with a wish
Not just today But all the days after.	Ends with a wish

On the other end of a spectrum is the "disguised" wish which uses a less direct (and usually longer) approach to conveying a greeting. This Christmas sentiment is a good example:

Take the crackling crispness Of a cold December night, Add two generous parts of snow That clothes the earth in white,	Wish disguised as recipe
Garnish it with shining bells And candles' golden light, Add a dash of friendship, Serve with memories shining bright—	
It's a good, time-tested recipe, And may it play a part In bringing all the happiness Of Christmas to your heart.	End with wish

Formula 8: Give it action!

Action catches the reader's attention and livens up the message. This sentiment begins by describing an action, usually something the sender does that has a bearing on the sending of the wish. This may lead to more wishing or a compliment. For example:

First I made a wish Then tucked inside	The action
A world of affection And loving pride For the two of you, Mother and Dad—	Leading to compliment
The very best parents Anyone ever had!	Compliment continues

or

Did you know I saw a wishing well And tossed a penny in it?	The action
I did! And wished your birthday Would be happy—every minute!	A wish
And then I threw another in Especially for YOU So, make a wish now of your own And know it's coming true!!	More wishing (indirectly)

There you are—eight models around which you can build greeting card sentiments. They are intended to help you get started with your messages, and the more you use them, the more helpful they will be to you. But remember, they are just models; they are not the goal, only the means to it.

The Inside Left

You can enhance your ideas by making use of what the industry calls the "inside left." This is copy that is printed inside the card on the left-hand page. An inside left may be one or more lines of poetry or it may be prose of varying lengths. The words or thought pertain to the card's sentiment on the inside right. The inside left is not the *message* of the card; it is the *highlighting* of the message, the *emphasizing* of it, the *strengthening* of it. For example, Elizabeth Barrett Browning's sonnet beginning, "How do I love thee?" might be quoted in part as the inside left for a husband, wife, or sweetheart card that expresses the love of the sender. James Whitcomb Riley's "He is just away" has been used as the inside left for sympathy cards. Quotations from the Bible, echoing a thought in the sentiment, are often used. And if you want to use a quote but can't find one, you can write your own:

Cover:	IN SYMPATHY
Inside left:	Those dearest to our hearts live on in memories. Author Unknown
Inside right:	May memories be your comfort today and your strength for tomorrow.

Don't be upset by being "Author Unknown." Card companies don't usually print the name of staff or free-lance writers; it doesn't lend the air of profundity to a quote that "Author Unknown" does! Inside lefts can be a bit more poetic than sentiments are, so if you need to rid yourself of poetic tendencies, this is the place to do it.

Writing a really good conventional card is a challenge—to make the sentiment fresh, original, and sendable when countless others have preceded it on the editor's desk and in the card shops.

CHAPTER 5

Soft Touch Cards

It has been more than a decade since a concept called "Soft Touch" revolutionized the industry with a new flavor of youthful sincerity in greeting cards, books and a multitude of related products. In that period, Soft Touch cards have affected and influenced the style of other kinds of greeting cards and the industry as a whole.

Initially these cards were sold in racks or spinners that were separate from conventional and other cards, because they were written and designed exclusively for a youth market. Now you will find Soft Touch displayed with conventional cards because the designing and writing of these cards has broadened to make them suitable for a wide range of senders and recipients. Many conventional designs carry sentiments with a Soft Touch flavor, and many Soft Touch messages are borrowed directly from conventional rhymed verses that have been distilled into prose.

Soft Touch cards are closely akin to conventional cards. Both are serious cards that convey emotions, but the *way* they do it makes the difference. It's the difference between the mildness of cologne (conventional) and the potency of perfume (Soft Touch). Both are good; they just differ, that's all.

Take a look at the basic differences:

The market—While Soft Touch cards are still suitable for the younger market, they are now also popular with the "young at heart" card buyers who are rather sophisticated, usually well educated, and quite sentimental. These cards are exchanged among contemporaries—contemporaries at least in their thinking. They are sent because the buyer wants to say something, but not out of a sense of obligation to acknowledge a birthday, express sympathy, or concern for illness. While conventional cards are often sent as a result of varying degrees of traditional social practice or pressure, Soft Touch cards are more likely to be sent on impulse to express a feeling or observe a special event in a very close relationship.

The appearance—Soft Touch cards usually rely on mood photography to show their directness—couples in love strolling hand-in-hand along a beach, a dramatic sunrise or sunset, the moon reflected in the ocean, the enlargement of a flower, a lonely figure silhouetted against the sky. The artwork does not use frills and is as direct as the sentiment.

The sentiment—Soft Touch messages are much more personal and straightforward than those on the average conventional card. They are usually in prose, although rhyme may be used if it adds impact to the message. They are often (but not always) short, ranging from three or four words to twenty-five or thirty. They should be totally free of padding and completely informal and conversational. The wording is contemporary, lively, and never archaic or old-fashioned.

Perhaps the difference between conventional and Soft Touch cards can best be illustrated by these two examples. First, a conventional message:

> I miss you more with every day,
> I'm always thinking of you,
> But the way I miss you is nothing . . .
> Compared to how I LOVE you!

Now the Soft Touch message:

> I miss you as I love you . . .
>   completely!

See how direct and personal it is? There's not one wasted word and the message carries a lot of emotional impact.

SENDING SITUATIONS

As with any other card, you should start the writing process with a *sending situation* and an idea. The majority of Soft Touch cards are romantic. They are designed and written for people in various stages of a love relationship to send to one another on a variety of occasions and for different reasons. There are some cards, for example, intended for early in a man/woman relationship simply to express the happiness the sender feels. Here are two such cards:

> All my yesterdays seem so ordinary
>   all my nows so very special
>   all my tomorrows promise dreams . . .
>   . . . since you came into my life.

or

> My world is a very special place . . .
>   . . . now that I share it with you

As the relationship grows closer the messages become more intimate:

> Of all the places in the world I like . . .
>   . . . I like being in your arms best.

> or

> I'm yours, you're mine, we're ours . . .
>   . . . and I'm so glad we belong to each other.

Finally, when the feelings deepen to full-fledged love, the messages are extremely sentimental:

> You are my lover, my life, my friend . . .
>   . . . and I love you.
> Today . . . tomorrow . . . forever . . .
> I love you.

Soft Touch messages have their embellishments, too, especially when the "deep love" stage is involved. These usually take the direction of exaggeration rather than poetic imagery (which often appears in conventional sentiments). Here's an example in which the writer used the "improbable" formula:

> If I could be with you every second
>   of every day . . .
>   . . . I still wouldn't have enough time to
>   love you.

Sending situations are not limited to lovers. Many Soft Touch cards are suitable for friends and close relatives as well. Some even fit the "anyone to anyone" situation, as does this all-purpose birthday card:

May your whole world be happy . . .
. . . especially today.
Happy Birthday

Soft Touch cards to friends frequently take on a more personal tone than do those on conventional designs. Here's an example:

There aren't many friendships as special as ours . . .
. . . but then, not many friends are as special as you!

You will find sending situations in a Soft Touch line which you are not likely to see covered by conventional cards. For example, there are cards for "someone who has been like a sister to me"; "welcome" cards for people moving into a neighborhood or starting a new job; or "apology" cards for misunderstandings between lovers or close friends. The simplicity and directness of the writing in these cards gives them added sincerity. A classic apology, for example, reads:

Sorry . . .
. . . we really know how to hurt
one another, don't we?

Develop an awareness of situations in which people, particularly younger people, communicate with one another; then try your hand at helping them communicate via the written word. As always, researching the card racks is a good way to become familiar with different types of messages, but if you want to write Soft Touch, don't just stop there. Research life.

IDEAS

Unlike many conventional cards which rely on elaborate sentiment/design tie-ins for their idea, Soft Touch cards are basically very simple. Like rock or country and western music, the wording is direct and free of obscure imagery. There's no talk in these cards about friendships being sheltering trees or pansies standing for thoughts. Successful Soft Touch cards relate to routine activities in everyday life, an act as simple as closing your eyes, as in this message:

> We're never far apart . . .
> . . . I simply close my eyes and there you are.

Even day-to-day surroundings have been used as starters for a Soft Touch card idea, as in this one:

> In the clamor of the crowded days
> or the silence of the lonely nights . . .
> . . . I miss you!

Many times you will find that "tuning in" to human nature will provide you with a wealth of ideas. Here's an example from a Mother card:

> For all the times I should have said it,
>   but didn't . . .
>   . . . thanks, Mom!   Happy Birthday!

Many popular Soft Touch cards are based on a long, rhymed conventional card, and the sentiments in your successful conventional verse can be an excellent source of ideas for Soft Touch cards. Extract the main message from some of your conventional rhymed messages and try writing it in prose. Here's an example of how it can be done. First, the conventional sentiment:

You make everything happy
Whatever you do,
That's why it's so grand
To be good friends with you.

What is the thought here? That the recipient is actively responsible for the good friendship the sender and recipient share. With that in mind, it's only a short step away from a message like this:

I like sharing friendship with you . . .
. . . because you make friendship worth sharing.

When you tackle a longer conventional sentiment, you may have to do some selective editing in order to shorten it. In other words, pick only the meatiest ideas to transform into a Soft Touch message. Here's an example:

A WEDDING WISH
As you look at one another
May you treasure what you see,
May the sound of laughter echo
Through each happy memory;
May your love keep on increasing,
May your hopes and dreams come true,
And may life always be as beautiful
As this day is for you.

The first four lines are pleasant, but a bit too poetic, especially for Soft Touch, so concentrate on the last four. Senders of Soft Touch like their messages to be realistic and would shy away from "dreams come true." The last step is to convert them to prose. Here's one way:

> May your love keep growing,
>   your hopes and dreams become reality
>   and life always be as wonderful for you
>   as it is today.

A shorter approach might be to say:

> May your life together
>   and your love
>   always be as beautiful
>   as it is today.

After rewriting this conventional verse, look at the originals again and then at your "rewrites" to see what new ideas might spring from them. The result might be something like this:

> May you *two* always be *one*
>   in love
>   in laughter
>   in living.

All three messages are salable, but the last one is most likely to excite an editor because in addition to sendability, it offers freshness—and the good old "rule of three." The best advice is to try several approaches before you settle on your favorite, even if you're satisfied with your first effort.

WORDS

Once you have chosen a sending situation and an idea, you are ready to put your thoughts into words—Soft Touch words. It's important to make every word count, to make every word conversational, and to make every word carry the greatest possible emotional impact. Of course it's not easy; that's why editors are willing to pay so well for Soft Touch writing.

Make every word count. Take the time to make your messages as brief as possible. If you've written something like this:

> Hardly a day in the week goes by that
> I don't think about you . . .
> . . . and so I'm sending this card to let you know it!

you should go back over it and remove the padding. Expressions like "so I'm sending you this card . . ." are unnecessary, no matter *what* kind of card you're writing; they can ruin a Soft Touch card. "Hardly a day in the week goes by . . ." is not only unnecessary, it also borders on being downright wishy-washy. The whole phrase can be boiled down into the useful word "often." Finally, instead of using the negative word "don't," take a positive approach. Your edited version, then, should look something like this:

> I think of you often . . .
> . . . and I wanted you to know it.

There are certain words that carry enough emotional impact so that they don't need a lot of weaker words around them; in fact, their impact may be actually lessened by association with unimportant words. Here's an example of such a "burial":

> Of all the words in the dictionary,
> *friendship* is one of the most wonderful . . .
> Of all of the friendships in the world,
> ours is one of the greatest!

The thought is beautiful, but the writing has done damage to the idea. The most important word—friendship—appears after seven other unimportant words. The second most im-

portant word doesn't appear at all—the magic word "you."
"Ours" is personal, but it lacks the impact of "you." There are
two other damaging words here, too—"wonderful" and
"greatest." They introduce hyperbole—a dangerous thing on
a Soft Touch card. There are three important words necessary
to do this idea justice—*friendship, word,* and *you.* Put them
together in a way they will have maximum impact:

> Friendship . . . what a nice word
> You . . . what a nice friend!

Keep in mind that Soft Touch cards are straightforward,
outspoken, and sincere. Card buyers don't want such super-
latives as:

> You're perfect, Mom . . .
> . . . absolutely perfect!

Moms may be nice, but they are not perfect!
Here is an example of the more sincere message that would
be preferable:

> You're a really great mom . . .
> . . . I'm glad you're mine!

Make every word conversational. Resist the temptation to
use poetic or flowery language on these cards. Instead of
saying:

> Just one birthday is too brief a time
> to contain all the happiness you're being wished . . .
> . . . so, have a happy *always!*

Get to the point much more quickly with:

> Have a bright and beautiful birthday . . .
> . . . and a million happy tomorrows.

Avoid contrived and unfamiliar expressions like "have a happy always." All they do is confuse your reader.

Coining your own words, especially adjectives, is risky business. The results may seem clever at the time, but they often look and sound contrived to the reader. Rather than doing something like this:

> Have a free-as-a-breeze, do-as-you-please . . .
> . . . happy, happy birthday!

you're better off using conversational wording like this:

> Wishing you love and laughter,
>   sunshine and flowers . . .
>   . . . and a year full of happy hours!

When you are using a conversational style, keep in mind *who* the speaker is. Remember that a very large percentage of buyers are women. Don't have them use language that is unsuitable, as in this wording on a Thank You card:

> Kindness is the oil that takes the friction
>   out of life.

It might fit on a calendar destined for the wall of a service station garage, but not on a woman's greeting card.

"Conversational" reflects thinking as well as talking. Soft Touch senders want their cards to mirror their outlook on life, and in the 1980's you simply will not be able to sell cards like this one:

> To my husband—my provider, protector
>   my friend, my Christmas . . .
>   . . . every day of the year!

"Provider and protector" just aren't compatible in a society where nearly half of all wives are working and doing much of the "providing" themselves. These are not terms younger wives and many older women would use—they would prefer something more like this:

> You are my husband . . .
>   my joy, my song,
>   my love, my Christmas . . .
>   . . . every day of the year!

The *who* is an important influence on the language you select for a Soft Touch card. Since young people are an important segment of the market, contemporary language must be used; expressions must be timely and familiar to the under-30 crowd. Here are some examples:

> My life needs someone like you, someone to talk with,
> to understand, *to make the clouds go away* . . .
>   . . . someone to love as I love you.

> or

> In a world where it seems hard to find someone who cares
>   and understands, I'm so grateful to have found you . . .
>   . . . for through you, *I have found myself.*

Make every word carry the greatest possible emotional impact. Since very few Soft Touch messages are written in rhyme, there's no need for padding. But brevity alone won't do the job. The few words you choose must strike an emotional chord with your reader. Look at this message:

> You're there . . . and I'm here . . .
>   . . . and I hate it!

It's brief, but for emotional impact, the writer has chosen a "downer" word—hate. Hate conjures up an emotion, but not the one we want here. The sender wants the recipient to know how much she misses him, with no possibility of misunderstanding. A better ending, then, would be this:

> You're there . . . and I'm here . . .
> . . . and in between is loneliness.

"Loneliness" requires no interpretation, and since the recipient probably shares the emotion, it expresses the message beautifully.

Use the words that appeal to the senses—"the sound of your laughter," "the touch of your hand," "the sight of your smile," and so on. Notice how a writer appeals to the senses in this message:

> On the day when my longing for you becomes an ache,
> I look up at the sky and wish I could be the wind . . . to touch your face, and ruffle your hair . . .
> . . . and whisper to you late at night.

To sum up: Soft Touch cards should be "meaty" and really say something. They should communicate on an emotional level that indicates the kind of impact a sender and recipient have on one another. Above all, they should express real feelings in a fresh, modern, emotional, and true-to-life style of writing.

CHAPTER 6

Cute, Informal, and Clever Cards

HERE ARE three greeting card sentiments. They all say approximately the same thing, and yet they fall into three distinct categories as far as card companies are concerned. How do they differ? In subtle but important ways.

Just a card to help me show ya
How very glad I am to know ya!   CUTE

Just a little reflection . . .
. . . of my warmest affection!   INFORMAL

Nobody's perfect . . .
. . . but you sure come close!   CLEVER

CUTE—A cute card is the "light" end of a conventional line. The design has one or more "action" figures (cute birds, animals, children), but the action is not emphasized, and there is no particular tie-in between the sentiment and the design. The writing is light, chatty, and usually short. It is frequently in rhymed verse. Note that the cute example above could be used with nearly *any* lighthearted design, from an animal to a little girl.

70

INFORMAL—An informal card is a "bridge" between the conventional and the humorous card. The design involves cute characters in rather limited situation humor, and the sentiment ties in with that situation. In the above example, the design would need to be a cute girl looking into a mirror, or a kitten gazing at her reflection in a pool. Informal cards may be in rhyme or prose, usually the latter.

CLEVER—A clever card is a lighthearted humorous card, brief, feminine in tone, and with a definite sentiment-design tie-in. Clever cards are more sophisticated than cutes and informals and may use adult women in the designs in place of the cute girls found on the others. The sentiments are short and may or may not rhyme.

As you can see from the three definitions, design plays a critical role in these cards, so it becomes necessary to start thinking visually as well as verbally when you work on them. If you have some artistic talent, good; but a lack of it should not prevent you from writing and selling some good cute, informal or clever cards. You can *write* a description of the design you have in mind alongside the sentiment, or attach a design "lead" taken from a magazine, newspaper, cartoon, etc., to help explain your idea.

Now look at each type in greater detail.

CUTE

Cute cards are intended to appeal to women and are designed for a strictly female market. They are often used as juvenile cards, too, for young girls from age eight into their teens, who are simply too "grown up" for obviously juvenile cards.

One good way to start writing cute cards is to let your thoughts bounce along to a lighthearted meter. Once you have a "sendable" thought, try a swift-paced meter (anapestic — is good) and you're sure to come up with something sprightly. Another way is to play around with some cute rhyme words, some breezy expressions, or some friendly, sincere compliments—anything that will keep your message lighthearted. Cute cards are no place to introduce weighty matters or complex sentiments. Here are some examples, starting with a light and lively meter:

> Here are loads of good wishes
>   especially for you
> For today and tomorrow
>   and all the year through!

Here is an example of an industry best seller that uses colloquial language:

> A little card I went and boughtcha . . .
> . . . to let you know I ain't forgotcha!

Then, a well-known breezy expression, in this sentiment:

> Who hopes you're feeling better?
> Who's sending you this HI?
> Who thinks about you often?
> ME . . . MYSELF . . . AND I!

Not all cutes must be in rhymed verse. Prose can be handled in a light, bouncy way, too. Here's an example—it doesn't rhyme, but it has a nice, sprightly meter:

> Of course I remembered your birthday!
> You're too nice to ever forget!

Since cute cards are aimed at a women's market, use plenty of feminine rhymes. They'll give your sentiment some extra bounce:

> Nothin' fancy, nothin' clever
> Just thinkin' aboutcha as much as ever
> And thought this might just help to show ya
> How very glad I am to know ya!

What about the *language* in cute cards? The examples just shown use contractions like "boughtcha/forgotcha," "'cause" and the ungrammatical "ain't" and "went and boughtcha." Good or bad? Generally speaking, the more conversational you make cute cards, the better they sell. "Cutesy" can be appropriate on cute designs as long as the language isn't affected or outdated. Here's an example of overdone "cutesy":

> Golly, if you only knew
> 'Zactly what I think of you
> You'd blush and swaller once or twice
> 'N say, "Gee whiz . . . am I THAT nice?"

The best rule of thumb is to listen to people talk and then use the most conversational vocabulary. Lots of people still use "'cause" in place of "because" . . . but whom do you know who says "'zactly" for "exactly"?

INFORMALS

Perhaps the major difference between informal and cute cards is the degree of the sentiment-design tie-in. Cute cards often rely simply on the lighthearted "feel" of cuteness to set the tone for the sentiment. There is usually no attempt to write the message around a character or a situation. Informal cards, on the other hand, get much of their strength from a good illustration with a strong situation and an appropriate tie-in message. For example, a piece of art showing two girls sharing an ice cream soda might have this sentiment:

Friendship is a treat for two . . .
Lucky me for knowing you!

Tone is very important. Because informals serve as a "bridge" between conventional and humorous, they often require a more sophisticated tone than cutes. While informals are usually suitable to send to people of all ages, they tend to attract adult senders and recipients. This is often accomplished by making reference to topics, slogans, mottoes, songs, and clichés familiar to adults. This message, for example, relies on the sender/recipient knowing an old song, "I'm Forever Blowing Bubbles":

(Art: animal blowing bubbles)
I'm forever . . .
. . . thinking of you
(and enjoying it, too!)

This card relies on an adult vocabulary:

(Art: male sheep thinking of female sheep)
I'm thinking of ewe.

This last example introduces something that makes informal cards stand apart from cutes—subtlety. This can be both a good device and a dangerous one because if you make your message too subtle, you lose customers. The connection between wording and design should be a one-step link . . .

not a two- or three-step journey. For example, this card which is illustrated with a teddy bear says simply:

Consider yourself hugged!

Here are the steps expected of the customer looking at this card:

1. Identify the character as a teddy bear.
2. Determine that teddy bears are something children and some adults like to hug.
3. Decide that sending a teddy bear is like sending a hug (even though it is people who hug teddy bears . . . not vice versa).

By the time the customer has made this many associations, she may have long since tired of the card. On the other hand, another card showing a bluebird amidst a flock of geese, goes right to the heart of that matter and says:

You're a rare bird!

The customer simply has to recognize:

1. The bluebird is different from the flock.
2. So is the recipient of the card.

Go back to the teddy bear design for a minute. Here is a way you can write for this design and avoid being too subtle:

I could hug you to pieces . . .
. . . then hug all the pieces

The message now stands by itself. Its play is on "pieces" more than "hug," and the card makes sense even if the customer doesn't associate teddy bears with hugging. If she does make that association, then it's a bonus for her.

CLEVER CARDS

Clever cards are more humorous than informals. The humor, however, is gentler, though not necessarily less funny than that found on humorous cards. Clever cards often go after the "Awww" rather than the "Ha ha" response. Here's an example:

> (Art: hen in nest, knitting)
> To MOM . . .
> . . . who made OUR NEST THE BEST!
> HAPPY MOTHER'S DAY

Clever cards will make greater use of sophistication (or pseudosophistication) than humorous or informal cards, as evidenced by this card:

> (Art: woman nearly covered by roses)
> I wish you a bed of roses . . .
> Without the damn thorns!
> FEEL BETTER SOON

While puns are primarily used in the humorous line, properly handled, they can be successful in clever cards, too. Here are two examples:

> (Art: animated apple core)   (Front)
> You're fabulous . . . right down to the core!   (Inside)

> (Art: jar of preserves)   (Front)
> Happy Birthday . . .
> To someone who's well-preserved!

When you use puns in clever cards, be sure to keep them feminine in appeal. Remember, you're after a smile, not a belly-laugh. On the other hand, don't give a woman words to say that she won't feel comfortable with. Women are not fond of "baby talk" and would probably reject a pun like this:

> (Art: basket of animated strawberries)
> I love you BERRY MUCH

Rhyming is a good device to use on clever cards, especially when you stray from the ordinary. This rhyme scheme made a good card:

> (Art: woman talking to man)
> Just between the TWO of us . . .
> I really like the YOU of us!

As with every kind of card, the first step in writing cute, informal, and clever greetings is to get an idea. There are three good starting points: 1) a design; 2) a word; 3) a message. Or you may choose any combination of these to start you off.

DESIGN

Nearly anything can be a design-starter for these cards, and you will find that one single design idea may provide several sentiment ideas. Take sunshine, for example. Look at some of the ways it can be converted into cards:

> *Informal*
> > (Art: Sun with breezes, birds, etc.)
> > A bright and breezy "Hi" . . .
> > To a warm and sunny friend!
>
> *Informal*
> > (Art: smiling sun)
> > I like your sunny smile!

Once you start your mind brainstorming around a design idea, don't turn it off just because you are working on cute cards at the time. If you have a good idea for a conventional sentiment, write it down and file it. Your sunshine design, for instance, might spark this inside left idea:

Cute

FOR A SPECIAL FRIEND

As growing things need sunshine,
As nature needs the spring,
Everyone needs the warmth and love
That only friends can bring.

While you have sunshine on your mind, check to see if it offers any humorous or studio ideas, and you might come up with a funny card like this good seller:

Clever

A million years from now the SUN will
swallow the EARTH . . .

. . . makes being sick seem kind of
insignificant, doesn't it?

When you come up with a good line for a design, don't stop. Play with the design for as long as it gives off "good vibrations." For example, suppose you are brainstorming a strawberry design, making note of all the things that relate to that particular fruit. Your list might look something like this:

Strawberry: shortcake, jelly, jam, ice cream, pie
ripe, pick, slice, eat, dessert
delicious, special, tasty, scrumptious
whipped cream, milk, sugar, cereal
red, green   spring, summer

Card ideas: Have a delicious birthday   (a scrumptious day)
              Glad I picked you for a friend
              Birthdays are like strawberries
              Extra sweet . . . that's you

From these, you are ready to put together some good sentiments:

Informal

         Friends are the strawberries   (Front)
         on the shortcake of life . . .

         . . . I'm glad I picked you   (Inside)
         for my friend.

(Art: little girl atop a giant strawberry)
Hi! (Front)
Have a scrumptious birthday!   (Inside)

See how it works? You not only have three good card ideas, you have a "brainstorm" list that might be explored for more card ideas later on. Don't throw it away; file it!

WORDS

Since words are your business, you'll find most of your ideas coming from words or phrases. When you're reading books, magazines, newspapers, advertisements or watching TV or movies or listening to the radio, train yourself to be on a constant search for words. Jot them down and file them, and you'll find your brainstorms will become much easier and more productive. Your thesaurus and rhyming dictionary can be helpful, too.

You will find at least three types of words or phrases very helpful in getting ideas for cute/informal/clever cards:

1. Clichés
2. Current, popular expressions
3. Everyday conversation

Clichés, of course, are well-known but usually overworked expressions which shouldn't find their way into your cards "as is." But as starters for fresh ideas, they can be valuable. For example, the expression, "In my book" might lead to this card:

In my book . . .
. . . there's no one any nicer than you!

And from the cliché "under lock and key" comes this idea:

Can't keep it under lock and key . . .
You're the only one for me!

The possibilities are as endless as the list of clichés all around you.

At the other end of the spectrum are current or popular expressions. It's important to choose words and phrases that are up-to-date. Don't try to be "hip" . . . just current. For example, from the popular expression "you're so together," might come this card:

The more we're together . . .
. . . the more I'm together!

Another timely phrase could lead to this get-well card:

How are things in your little corner
of the world?
Better, I hope! GET WELL SOON

Expressions like "Tiger," "Pussycat," "Macho," "Foxy," "Turkey," have become part of the national vocabulary and make good starters for greeting cards. While these may have great possibilities for humorous/studio cards, they are also good for some clever cards. In these cases, they may rely mostly on the cleverness of the art and say simply:

Happy Birthday . . . Tiger

Currently popular commercial products or public personalities in many cases are perfectly usable. Here are a couple of examples:

Sorry I forgot your birthday!
I must have a Teflon brain . . .
Nothing sticks to it!

What a smile! What sexy eyes!
What a body!
But enough about Burt Reynolds . . .
    Happy Birthday to YOU!

If you have any doubts about what products and which personalities are usable and which aren't, just go ahead and submit the idea. The editor will know which are suitable and publishable.

Everyday conversation will stimulate dozens of ideas for cute/informal/clever cards. Anything people say to one another can serve as a starting point. For example, the expression "Smile!" or "Keep smiling" has led to many a good greeting card. This one has been the most popular:

Smile!
Even if it's one of those days!

The term "Happiness is . . ." has spawned many card sentiments, too. Among them is this classic:

> Happiness is . . .
>   . . . having a friend like you
>   to wish a Happy Birthday to!

How many times have you heard a person say, "You know something?" Use it as a springboard to a greeting card, as in this example:

> You know something?
> Everything I like to do
> Is TWICE the fun when shared with *you*!

The possibilities are innumerable, and when you combine words from everyday conversation with everyday action in a design, you have some very salable informal/clever cards. One final example shows a little character running hard and shouting:

> Hey!!! You left something behind!
> ME!
> Have a wonderful trip

Sending situations will often determine the tone of a card and when you're doing your brainstorming for cute/informal/clever cards, take some time to list situations that are appropriate for card-sending from woman to woman. It may be as simple as a "thinking of you" situation that prompts a message like this:

> There's no special reason for sending you this card . . .
>   . . . I just thought you'd enjoy getting something that didn't
>   have to be paid by the 10th of the month!

What other situations occur in the lives of women, especially housewives and mothers, that might make a good clever card? For example, taking care of children prompted one writer to come up with this excellent seller:

> "Thappy Biff Hoo Foo Gooey Da Poo"
> That's "Happy Birthday"! I've been
>   home with the kids all day!

Sometimes even a feeling can prompt a sending situation—like the special good feeling you have when things are going your way, and there is someone in your life who contributes to your happiness. You feel good about life, you feel good about your friend, and you want to tell her so. The result may be a card like this one:

> Life is Great!
> . . . and *one* of my reasons is
>   *you're* my *friend*!

There are times when the *design* idea dictates the *sending situation* as well as the tone of the card. This frequently happens when the design employs "character art"—a well-known character used exclusively by a specific card company. The cartoon character Ziggy, an American Greetings staple, is a lovable loser, a hapless hero who seldom wins but always keeps trying, and so a card written with him in mind would have to be "in character" . . . like this one:

> Well, no one has claimed me for 30 days . . .
> . . . so I guess I'm yours!

By contrast, a card written with a Holly Hobbie design in mind would not carry that kind of humor. It might rely more on a sentiment/design tie-in, like this:

> (Art: Holly blowing candles on cake)
> Happy candle-blowing!

Every greeting card "character" has a personality—Hallmark's Betsey Clark girls, Rust Craft's "Rusty," Norcross's "W.C. Dog"—and each requires a specific kind of sentiment. The more you study their lines, the better you will understand their needs.

Can *you* submit material suitable for the personalities of these characters? Yes. In nearly every case, the artists do not write copy for their cards—it comes from staff and free-lance writers.

These are just some of the devices that can help you develop ideas for cute/informal/clever cards. Start with these and as you gain experience, you can develop techniques of your own. You'll find that these cards can be fun to write because you can play with words, rhymes, and pictures. Keep in mind the importance of design as well as sentiment and try to tie them together as a unit. Finally, work on these cards when you're in a cheerful mood. The results should look and sound as if you had fun writing.

 CHAPTER 7

Basic Formulas for Humor

WRITING humorous and studio cards looks easy, but it isn't. Humor is serious business, and should be approached as such. All humor fits into several basic formulas, and these formulas hold true whether you're writing studio or humorous cards. The treatment may vary, but the formulas remain the same.

Exaggeration—Enlarge an idea: go overboard, stretch the reader's imagination almost to the breaking point. Do the idea or the card up big! Don't be ashamed of telling a whopper! Some examples:

> Sorry I haven't written, but so many things
> have happened lately . . .
> . . . the Johnstown flood, the Chicago fire,
> The San Francisco quake . . .

or

> I LOVE YOU with all my HEART and SOUL,
> with IMMEASURABLE PASSION, with every FIBER of my
> BEING!!!
> No wonder I'm so pooped all the time!

Sometimes exaggeration is used in the design or size of a card. An oversized card is intrinsically funny, regardless of the formula used in the message. If you can combine design exaggeration with exaggeration of the humor, you may really come up with a winner.

Understatement—Underplay a gag; reduce it in size or scope; pretend that what is happening is of much smaller importance than it is. Understatement is simply exaggeration in reverse:

> I think of you in all my sober moments!
> . . . last week I thought of you TWICE

Sometimes understatement, combined with an exaggerated design, makes the card funny because of the obvious contrast. For example: the cover design shows a character hanging by chains in a dark dungeon, cobwebs partially covering him. The situation is an obvious exaggeration, but the message inside reads:

> Sorry I haven't written
> but nothing much has happened lately

That is effective understatement.

Word Play—This is a formula you can have fun with because it's a writer's dream, playing with words. Probably the most obvious form of word play is the *pun*, often considered to be the purest form of humor. It is most often used in the humorous line, but by making it more outrageous than usual, you can use it in the studio line, too. An example is a studio card with a picture of a Koala bear on the cover. On the inside, it reads:

> When it comes to nice friends . . .
> . . . you Koala-fy

Another card shows a picture of an animated yam. It reads:

> Know who's crazy about you?
> I yam!

A more up-to-date card combines a pun with an old "knock-knock" joke:

> Knock, knock! Who's there?
> POLICE! Police who?
> . . . POLICE write me that letter you owe me!

Repetition is another form of word play that gets a laugh. Here's an example:

> Ours is a strange and wonderful relationship . . .
> . . . you're strange and I'm wonderful!

Also, try using clichés or popular phrases or idioms literally, and you can produce some funny results, as in the following:

> You make my heart throb . . .
> . . . and my ear ring . . . and my shower stall . . . and my teeter totter . . . and my drum roll . . . and my kitchen sink . . . and my birch bark . . . and my ginger snap . . . etc.

While you're playing with words, try substituting a word or words in a well-known phrase, and you will open up an unlimited number of possibilities. This is done successfully on this get-well card for a man:

> I hear you've taken a turn for the . . .
> . . . NURSE!
> Keep it up and get well quick

Fracture the language now and then, and you'll get a laugh. This could be in the form of a malapropism (a confusion of two words somewhat similar in sound but different in meaning) or simply some distorted grammar intended to strengthen your word play:

> You're my favorite DO-GOODER . . .
>   . . . because you DO IT GOODER than anybody!

Rhyme, when handled well, can get a laugh. While rhyming is ordinarily used more in humorous than studio cards, if you're tricky enough you can come up with a popular studio. Here's a classic:

> To the hostess
> with the mostess . . .
>   . . . a toastess!

Truth formula—Telling the truth has resulted in a number of successful cards. Here you might make a "true" statement in such a naive way that it changes from "straight" to humorous.

> It's your birthday and I'm going to say
> something that might sound silly . . .
>   . . . "Belly Button!"
>   (I *told* you it might sound silly!)

Sometimes the *more* truth you put in a message, the funnier it becomes:

> This card does more than wish you a Happy Birthday!
>   . . . it also opens and closes and rides around
>   in an envelope.

Misunderstanding—When you use this formula, you are deliberately misunderstanding or misinterpreting a familiar expression or idiom. It's a successful device used by many night club and TV comedians. Here's how it works:

> I couldn't decide what to get you for your birthday . . .
> how does a new JAGUAR sound?
> > VAROOM . . . VAROOM!!
> > (anyhow, Happy Birthday)

Many combinations are possible with this formula, both with sentiment themes and other formulas. For example, you can combine it with the *Word Play* approach and come up with this gag:

> (picture of a European old-country peasant)
> Know what *this* is?
> . . . it's your Birthday PEASANT!!

Sarcasm—This is a handle-with-care formula, but when you use sarcasm right, you can produce some excellent card ideas. You can ridicule a weakness or idiosyncrasy of the recipient, but it should be tempered with implied admiration on the part of the sender:

> Did you know there are over 312 brands of beer
> > brewed in the United States alone?
> > . . . yes, I figured you did!

The classic card using this theme has the word SEX in big, bold letters on the card's cover. Inside, it reads:

> Now that I have your attention . . . Happy Birthday!

Surprise—Nearly all the humor involves surprise; you pull out all the stops and go to the unexpected so sharply that the reader *has* to laugh. There are several ways to achieve surprise, ranging from the irreverent to the irrelevant. An example of the irreverent shows a scene with carollers singing:

> "It came upon a midnight clear . . ."
> . . . look out! Here it comes again!
> MERRY CHRISTMAS

As for the irrelevant, here's an example:

> I've been keeping something from you . . .
> HUMPTY DUMPTY was PUSHED!

CHAPTER 8

Humorous Cards

A HUMOROUS card is built on "down to earth" humor that ranges from corny to funny. It is humor everyone can under-stand and enjoy—the same kind of humor you will find in cartoon strips like "Blondie" or in the routines of comedians like Bob Hope. There is little attempt at sophistication here, and this is where humorous and studio cards part company. There is an old industry rule of thumb that sums it up: "You will never lose sales by being too obvious!" The humor should be simple, understandable, and comfortable.

ART—Humorous cards use art that is uncomplicated, friendly, appealing, and ageless. There is usually a Disney-like quality about the funny animals or human characters used in humorous cards. These characters are quickly recog-nizable and their express purpose is to enhance the humor in the wording. There is usually a strong design-sentiment tie-in on humorous cards.

MARKET—Humorous cards appeal to a wider market than do studio cards. Because of their simple approach to humor, many of these cards are suitable for sending to people as young as nine or ten. The timelessness of the humor also makes these cards appealing to the over fifties. Although women are the prime buyers of humorous cards, many of these are aimed at men as well. The market for humorous cards is basically unsophisticated, but it's a market with a sense of humor.

Length is a major difference between humorous and studio cards. This is not just because of the difference in the type of humor each delivers, but because of the wider range of design and size options available in humorous cards. In these cards, novelty mechanicals, multiple folds, and booklets can utilize longer copy.

The elements in humorous cards are similar to those in studios—basic sentiment themes and humor formulas work well for both.

But in many instances, the starting point is different. In writing humorous cards, you are not simply going for a laugh; you are trying for a complete "package"—sentiment, design, and idea. Here are some good starting points:

Start with a design idea. Begin with a visual idea as well as a verbal one, because appearance is a vital part of a humorous card; that's why these cards are often called "illustrated cards." As a writer, you naturally think in terms of words, but when writing humorous cards, you must try to visualize the kind of design that will complement the words and get your message across. Try starting your thought process with an animal—say, a skunk. Brainstorm words associated with skunk (stinker, scent, "scentimental," sniff, etc.), and see which will best help get your message across. The finished product may be something like this:

Happy Birthday to SWEET l'il you . . .
. . . from SCENT-imental me!

or

Just want to remind you you're a year older . . .
. . . ain't I a STINKER?

Word play is just one approach. For another, you might take a picture of a baby or a wild animal and add an appropriate caption—one that matches the expression on the subject and conveys the message you have in mind. An example would be a close-up of a cute baby, with these lines:

I remembered your birthday . . .
. . . ain't I ADORABLE?

Another example would be a photo of a mean-looking gorilla with these lines:

Have a happy birthday . . .
. . . or ELSE!

Start with a rhyme. A great many humorous cards are written in rhyme, and the rhyme itself contributes much of the humor. Here's one example:

ANOTHER BIRTHDAY? Well,
We're sure a long way from *innocent purity* . . .
. . . but we've still lots of time before *social security*!

That card can take any number of design approaches and still be funny. On the other hand, you might come up with something like this, which would require a specific design—a character in a hospital gown:

You there! You in the NIGHTY!
. . . let's hurry and get well quick . . . ALL RIGHTY?

Sometimes the rhyme is funny *and* says all there is to say in the message, as in this case:

> Valentine, if you wanna SNUGGLE . . .
> . . . I won't STRUGGLE!

And who says you have to stop with two rhymes? Sometimes three rhymes are better:

> Happy Anniversary to SISTER
> and the MISTER
> who couldn't RESIST 'ER!

Not everything in your rhyming dictionary will lead to a good humorous card, but sometimes when you're stuck for an idea, a spin through it will provide a good starter.

And remember, a good rhyme won't get you off the hook if you don't have a sendable message to put it with. You may get a laugh from an editor on this one, but you won't make a sale:

> Merry Christmas to a fine PLUMBER
> Thanks for keeping us from the TYPHUS
> And the GERMS that tried to KNIFE US!

Start with words. Sometimes a word or a collection of words will prompt card ideas. These may be in the form of puns, common expressions, word switches, or nothing more than simple words which provide a creative spark.

Puns are probably the most often-used form of word play in the humorous card line. They are funny, easy to understand, and provide excellent design ideas. Fortunately, too, the worse the pun, the better the public seems to like it. Editors feel no shame at all in publishing something like this:

(bunny design)
EARS to ya . . .
. . . with best wishes for an EGGSeptional Easter!

Or this:

Pardon the BALONEY . . .
. . . but aren't you a WEENIE bit older?

But card lines can't live on puns alone, and there is a limit to how many an editor can use in his line. Try some and submit them . . . but don't try to make a living writing only puns.

Popular phrases have been starting points for some excellent cards. Expressions in common use, like "hang in there," "keep smiling," and "better late than never" are naturals for this purpose. It's a good idea to keep a file of such phrases or sayings as you hear or read them. You'll find that going over these produces lots of card ideas. Here are some examples:

(3 monkeys)
Hear no evil, speak no evil, see no evil . . .
. . . of course that leaves DO NO EVIL wide open!
Live it up and have a happy birthday

On your birthday, if you don't do anything
ILLEGAL, IMMORAL or FATTENING you'll LIVE TO . . .
. . . regret it! So have a great birthday!

Word switches are also fun to write and fun to read. Here you take a common expression and switch it around, either using substitution or juxtaposition. An example:

Live it up! It may not add YEARS to your LIFE . . .
. . . but it will sure add LIFE to your YEARS!   Switch around

Another variation:

> Don't worry about birthdays,
> Just take 'em with a grin . . .
> It's true we may be HAS BEENS . . .   *Juxtaposition*
> . . . but just look where we HAS BEEN!

These aren't easy because they require more research and thought than other types of word play, such as puns. But editors love them, and the acceptance rate is very high.

Start with a gimmick. The humorous line is often referred to as a "gimmick" line because of its frequent use of attachments, novelty shapes and sizes, die-cuts, mechanical action, and unusual paper stocks. These make very good starting points for ideas.

Attachments are items, usually inexpensive, added to a card to help carry a gag or message. If you handle them right, the humor is 100% dependent on the attachment. For example:

> Want to see something SNAPPY?
> (rubber band attachment)

or

> For your wedding, here's a little something
>   to *feather your nest* . . .
> (feather attachment)

Both of the above use word play plus attachments to carry the message.

Here is another approach:

> (attachment: a difficult Chinese puzzle)
> While you're getting better,
>   here's something to OCCUPY YOUR MIND . . .
>   . . . or DRIVE YOU OUT OF IT!
> (character going mad trying to do puzzle)

Keep your attachments simple. Remember, most cards cost $1.00 or less, so the attachment must cost the manufacturer no more than one to five cents. Don't bother with bulky items like toys, breakable items like jewelry, or spoilable items like candy. Simple things like paper clips, erasers, extra paper, etc., stand a much better chance of being used than costly, complicated attachments.

Novelty shapes and sizes are good, inexpensive ways of adding value to your ideas. Sometimes they are used to enhance good word play, as in this case:

> (die-cut jar of jam)
> Don't worry about another birthday,
>   because without 'em . . .
>   . . . we'd sure be in a JAM!

Other times, they are the whole card:

> (die-cut pickle . . . no wording on cover)
> (inside) Bet you didn't expect a PICKLE
>   on your birthday card!

Good-selling sentiments have been written to cards die-cut in the shape of liquor bottles, beer steins, animals, upright pianos, buildings, boats, and just about every conceivable greeting card character. Sizes have varied from the very tiny to enormous $5.00 size cards, and sometimes the size or price of the card becomes the basis for the message. Here's an example from an oversized $2.00 card:

> I've never sent a Valentine as expensive as
>   this before . . .
>   . . . but then, I've never known anyone like YOU before!

Novelty die-cuts aren't limited to cut-out shapes. You can also work with ideas that have holes in the card, ranging from lots of holes (an "air-conditioned" card) to one with a single hole like this one:

> Place your finger in this hole,
> keep it in and open the card . . .
>   . . . you are now pointing to my favorite Mother!

Mechanical action was once a mainstay for humorous cards. Cards could pop up, stand up, move around and do just about everything but walk. With today's rising prices, these cards have become almost a thing of the past. If you can devise some good, simple mechanical action to enhance your word ideas, you might "click," but avoid the complicated. Here's an example of a card which depends completely on the mechanical action for its humor:

> Here's a little birthday card
> I think you'll find very *touching* . . .
>   (inside . . . no wording, just a mechanical
>   action of a large hand which reaches out
>   and touches the recipient)

Start with jokes. Many a good card owes its existence to a joke from another medium—a night club comic routine, TV sitcoms, magazine cartoons, or just a story told by a passing salesman. All of these can be made into salable greeting cards, if you can handle them skillfully. For example, a catty lady in a sitcom, talking to another woman about a mutual friend who was getting along in years, said, "Those dangerous curves of hers are nothing more than a lot of detours now . . ." This is funny, but it's negative. You can turn it into a compliment by pretending that the change isn't noticeable yet and come up with a birthday card that says:

> We don't need to worry about birthdays, Dearie . . .
> . . . until our DANGEROUS CURVES become EXTENDED
> DETOURS!
> (and we have miles to go before that happens)

From a college humor magazine comes the story of the grad whose parents promised him anything he wanted for his commencement gift—and now they're trying to gift-wrap a tavern. You could work this into a humorous graduation card, or it might be more appropriate for birthday, Christmas or New Year's greetings. Giving gifts is traditional for birthdays and Christmas, and since a drinking approach seems to be more widely used in birthday cards, a logical conversion to this greeting would be:

> Thought I'd get you what you wanted most
>   for your birthday . . .
> . . . but how do you wrap a SALOON?

The expression, "How do you wrap a . . ." can be used as the springboard for several messages. For instance, you could use the same opening with any of these punch lines:

> . . . but when I tried to wrap her, she slapped me!
> . . . but how do you gift wrap an orgy?
> . . . but how do you wrap THAT?

Notice how easy it is to use one gag as a starting point for a dozen different cards, most of which don't even resemble the original joke.

You should be aware of a difference in timing between telling a joke and writing a greeting card message. A "shaggy dog story" may be fine at a party and bring a lot of laughs, but the card customer will give your card about seven seconds of reading time. If you can't get your message and gag across on a card in that time, the card won't sell. Even a short spoken joke may be too long for a card gag. For example, on television, one person might say, "You know, you're more fun than a barrel of monkeys," to which a second man replies, "Well, I should certainly hope so—have you ever smelled a barrel of monkeys?" Funny? Yes. Greeting card material? Maybe—if you boil it down to something like this:

> Valentine, you're more fun than a barrel of MONKEYS . . .
> . . . you smell nicer, too!

Start with other card ideas. Once you've had a gag accepted, don't just file it away and forget it forever. Read it over and see if you can use it as a springboard to other card ideas. Say you had this card accepted:

> I spent four bits to send this
> And to show my high regard,
> So get well fast . . .
> . . . I don't have cash
> to buy another card!

The idea of the impoverished card sender spending his last half dollar on a greeting card is a good one. Where else could it be used? Birthday? Christmas? Both would probably work, so try Christmas:

> I thought of you at Christmas
> And to show my high regard
> I cashed my bonds and sold my stocks . . .
> . . . and purchased you this card!
> MERRY CHRISTMAS

Don't stop till you've exhausted every possibility. This same approach, for example, could probably develop into a good Halloween card:

> It's Halloween and I'm thinking of you
> So to show my high regard
> I went down to the cemetery . . .
> . . . and dug you up this card!

Start with a basic humor formula. The basic humor formulas work equally well in studio and humorous cards, so turn to them as you begin writing. Using the *exaggeration* formula, for example, plus a photo of a large stack of money and a complimentary theme can lead you to an idea like this one:

> (funny animal on top of a pile of money)
> This is the *million dollars* . . .
> . . . you look like on your birthday!

Combining the *truth formula* with some clever word play for a Wife Birthday card can yield an idea like this:

> To my WIFE, without whose loving concern
> I would remain UNfed, UNshaven, UNcaring,
> UNcooperative . .
> . . . and UNhappy!

Using the *Misunderstanding* formula, you might turn out copy like this:

> I hope you're not embarrassed by something
> WARM and MUSHY . . .
> Oatmeal

The possibilities of the basic "comparison" formula are practically limitless. Probably the most frequently used is "_____are like_____." There are plenty of examples of this, but the all-time classic is:

> Birthdays are like COCKTAILS . . .
> . . . the more you have, the more you wish you hadn't!

When you're stuck for an idea, this is an excellent starting point because it works for every occasion and caption.

> Hope your illness is like a PAYCHECK . . .
> . . . gone before you know it!

And comparison is an especially good approach for relative cards. Here is an example:

> BROTHERS are like EGGS
> Some are cracked
> Some are fried
> Some are hard-boiled, too
> But there's not a dozen anywhere
> Who are real GOOD EGGS
> . . . like YOU!

Other successful cards have compared fathers to automobiles (some have power, some have style . . . etc.); daughters to flowers (some are shy and modest, some bright and sunny . . . etc.); sisters to birthday presents (they come in all shapes and sizes); and so on.

Dialect gags were once a mainstay of humorous cards, and it was not uncommon to find messages written in the dialect of blacks, orientals, Italians, Germans, Spanish, hillbillies, etc. Today, under pressure from various groups that interpreted these as "slurs," and therefore offensive, these cards have virtually disappeared from the racks. Occasionally you will find a card using a simple word or expression of "foreign" origin, as in this graduation card:

> Wunderbar!
> How smart you are!
>   CONGRATULATIONS!

For the most part, whatever dialect is used on today's cards is from "obsolete" languages, or regional dialect, such as Western or Southern United States. Here are two examples:

SOME VIRTUOUS ADVICE FOR THANKSGIVING
Thou MUST eat with moderation
Thou MUST refuse all drinks
And if thou dost behave so well . . .
. . . Thou must be NUTS, methinks!

VALENTINE, When I see you
    my eyes start FLASHIN' . . .
. . . but that ain't anger—
    that there's PASSION!

Fortunately for the industry, St. Patrick's Day cards prove the exception to the no-dialect rule. Nearly all St. Patrick cards use Irish dialect. They sell well and nobody complains about them, so you can use as many "faith and begorras" as you want.

Using a *third party* to deliver your humor can give your cards some freshness. This device has been successful in both studio and humorous, but it is used most frequently in humorous. Here's an example from Christmas:

> I told SANTA what you want for Christmas
> and you know what he said?
>   HO HO HO!!

In that case, the ultimate me-to-you message is implied, because the sentiment stops with Santa Claus. In this next example, the sender re-enters the picture in time to deliver the message:

> SANTA thinks you're just about the
> nicest person . . .
> . . . South of the North Pole!
> (So do I!)

There are many messengers you can use for this approach—the Easter Bunny, Thanksgiving turkey, Halloween ghosts, Cupid for Valentine's Day, and so on.

Surprise, a formula used most successfully in studio cards, is used less in humorous, but handled right, it can be effective. In humorous cards, the set-up becomes more obvious and the punch line more of a relief than a surprise as in this example:

> SISTERS! You can have 'em ALL . . .
> . . . except MINE!

In that card, the recipient could be pretty sure she was going to receive a compliment, not a slam, although she was probably not sure the form it would take. In this next instance, the surprise is more complete because it comes in the middle of what appears to be an ordinary compliment:

> BROTHER, I already know you're witty,
> charming, intelligent, talented, kind
> and understanding . . .
> > I'll wait till after Christmas for
> > GENEROUS!

Because a humorous sentiment can be long, however, doesn't mean it should be "wordy." The longer the message, the more punch it should have, either in the form of clever rhyming or sustained humor. Here's an example:

> LOTS OF LOVE ON YOUR BIRTHDAY
> I'm not a TUBE of TOOTHPASTE
> or a SPONGE that's WRINGING WET!
> I'm not an ATOMIZER
> or a CLOTHESPIN, you can bet!
> I'm not a pair of PLIERS
> and I'm not a JUICY LIME
> But please, don't let that stop you . . .
> . . . GO ON, SQUEEZE ME ANY TIME!

Most long messages follow a "thread" throughout. The success or failure of the card depends on how strong that thread may be. Sometimes the thread is a good one, but the writer wears it thin by overworking it, as in this example:

> There are recipes for mixing drinks
> And frying crepe suzettes
> Recipes for canning pears
> And making ham croquettes
> There are recipes for baking pies
> And brewing Chinese tea
> Recipes for cooking stew
> And chicken fricassee
> But you two have the recipe
> For a happy married life
> By mixing one terrific guy
> With one terrific wife!
> HAPPY ANNIVERSARY

This is much too long; the reader will tire of the comparisons before reaching the end. A better approach would have been to make this an eight-line message, dropping the middle four lines. The next example shows how a long card can sound shorter by eliminating all but the absolute essentials:

WHAT IS A DAD?

A bread winner
   yard spinner
Faucet fixer
   cocktail mixer
Trainer
   explainer
Referee
   Ph.D.
Organizer
   economizer
Homework doer
   barbecuer
Chairman
   repairman
Physician
   electrician
Yes, a Dad is quite an all-around guy
With many things to do
And of all the dads throughout the world
The greatest one is YOU!

Writing humor isn't easy, but it can be very satisfying. More than any other type of writing, it requires imaginative ideas—lots of them. Much of your success in writing humorous and studio cards depends on your idea files. Set up a folder or group of folders and fill them with anything you feel will help you create funny cards—advertisements, artwork, words, phrases, other greeting cards, your own rejects, photos, books, calendars, jokes, etc. Keep adding to these files and get into the habit of working with them and using them often. This will give you a head start on any project or writing assignment you may tackle.

 CHAPTER 9

Studio Cards

THERE'S A FINE line between studio and humorous cards, but there is definitely a line. The two types of cards have as many differences as they have similarities—differences in humor, differences in art, and differences in market.

Studio cards go for the laugh, and like good professional comics, they will try just about anything to get it. They may be wry, caustic, whimsical, witty, dumb, funny, mean, irreverent, facetious, droll, risqué, topical, punny—whatever will make the reader laugh (or at least smile), and come up with the purchase price of the card.

But it's not true that "anything goes" in a studio card. Remember first that studios are *cards*, and they must therefore meet the basic requirements for all greeting cards: they must be sendable and have a me-to-you message. Beyond these basics, studio cards differ from others by reflecting a sophisticated, informed look at life. They appeal to a more intelligent market that includes a large number of well-educated, affluent and youthful (or young-at-heart) people.

As you write studio cards, you will try, naturally, to make them funny. The humor you will use can come from situations, special relationships between sender and recipient, surprise, outrage—dozens of sources. A joke by itself is rarely a good card, but with some help from a writer, it can be *converted* into a good card. Here's an example:

> A joke goes: (Cattily) "She doesn't have an enemy
> in the world! She's so old she's outlived
> them all!"

You can change that to make it a card:

> One thing you can say about being your age—
> you don't have an enemy in the world!
> . . . you've outlived them all!
> HAPPY BIRTHDAY, OLD FRIEND!

You can improve this message greatly by being good sport enough (and consequently less insulting) to include yourself in the kidding:

> There's a definite advantage in being our age—
> we don't have an enemy in the world!
> . . . we've outlived all of them!!!!
> HAVE A HAPPY BIRTHDAY

Many of the first studio cards were insulting and risqué, and there are writers today who still limit their repertoire to these two approaches. This is outdated thinking and can mean a loss in sales because there is such a wide range of themes available today. Even the insulting and risqué approaches have changed with time. The insults have become "slams." Slams are no longer mean; in fact, they are rarely really unkind. Most slams have a redeeming line that softens them:

> I believe in BIGFOOT,
> the LOCH NESS MONSTER,
> FLYING SAUCERS and YOU!
>   . . . I'm just naturally attracted to
>   WEIRD and UNUSUAL things!

It's a far cry from "drop dead," isn't it? The humor is simply good-natured kidding, and seldom is the recipient "put down" any worse than this:

> I always wanted to meet someone like you
> and now I finally have.
>   . . . big deal!

Risqué cards, for the most part, have been softened to "suggestive" and are still very much a part of every company's studio card offering; but except for a few of the small greeting card publishers who specialize in semi-pornography, suggestive humor is pretty much limited to innuendo or double meanings. Most major companies won't go much further than this:

> Happy Birthday, and remember
>   you're not old . . .
>   . . . until a QUICKIE takes
>   an HOUR and FIFTEEN MINUTES!

or this:

> It's your birthday, so go out and
>   have a great time—sing a little,
>   dance a little, drink a little . . .
>   . . . get a little!

You can still make sales with slams and suggestive cards, but there are many other equally strong themes to work with and you should be aware of all of them. Many are similar to what you will find in the conventional card line, but there are others which are applicable only to studio (and sometimes humorous) cards:

BIRTHDAY	FRIENDSHIP
Celebrating	Love
Drinking	Compliment
Age gags	Friend
Compliment	Missing you
Suggestive	Slam
No-gift gag	Thinking of you
Wish/gag	Suggestive
	No-occasion gag
	Romance
	Hello/hi

ANNIVERSARY	GET WELL
Wish/gag	Wish
Celebrating	Suggestive
Suggestive	Compliment
Compliment	Drinking
Philosophy	Gift gag
	Doctor gags

There are themes that are used exclusively in studio and humorous cards:

BIRTHDAY

Celebrating—Tells the recipient to "live it up" and enjoy the birthday not just by drinking (that's another theme) but by carousing in general:

Celebrate your birthday like a pendulum does . . .
    . . . Swing!

Drinking—Jokes about drinking, ranging from the pleasures to the problems. To many people, this is not a humorous topic, but it still gets laughs and sells.

> It's your birthday, so remember . . .
> happiness is an OLIVE . . .
>   . . . bounded on the north, south, east and west
>   by a martini!
> HAVE A FUN DAY

Age gags—Kid the recipient about growing older, sometimes directly, sometimes indirectly. These sell especially well when the sender is included in the gag:

> I won't say we're getting older, Kiddo . . .
>   . . . but we knew Howard Johnson when he had only
>   TWO FLAVORS!

Suggestive—Several approaches are available, often involving other themes, like age. An example:

> Another birthday? Well, you're not getting old . . .
>   . . . until your head makes a date your body can't keep!

No-gift gag—The sender apologizes for the price of the card or absence of a gift, blaming it on his lack of money:

> (Picture of an elephant) I'm sorry I
> didn't get you a more elaborate birthday card . . .
>   . . . but you know me—I work for peanuts!

Or, the sender goes to great lengths to tell why he is not giving the recipient a gift or to mislead her into thinking she *is* getting a gift:

Happy birthday to someone for whom I have only
the highest admiration . . .
. . . no present, just the highest admiration!

Wish/gag—The most salable of all the themes, usually, because it is a simple wish, free of limitations:

For Pete's sake, have a happy birthday!
. . . Pete has really been worried that you won't!

FRIENDSHIP

In the friendship line, there are these themes that differ from the studio birthday line and other non-humorous areas:

No-occasion gag—Impulse cards, sent for a multitude of reasons, ranging from keeping in touch to cheering up a hospital patient. The real message is usually added in handwriting by the sender:

"The Sky is Falling!!"
. . . please pass this along to
Goosey-Loosey!

Romance—Cards to send at various stages of a romance to describe the sender's feelings for the recipient:

In this day and age of vitamins, wonder drugs
and tranquilizers . . .
. . . I still need YOU!

GET WELL

Studio *get-well* cards differ greatly from conventional or cute. They are still encouraging to the patient and wish her a quick recovery, but they introduce a "whipping boy" to help the patient feel better—the doctor, nurse, hospital, etc.—or irreverent thoughts to help take the patient's mind off present problems:

Suggestive—Usually kidding the recipient about the inaction caused by the current (temporary) infirmity:

> There are a lot of things
> you can do in bed . . .
> . . . but you gotta get well first!

Drinking—These cards never imply that the recipient is ill because of a drinking problem. They usually imply that drinking will help speed recovery:

> Here are two ways for you to feel better fast . . .
> . . . gin and vermouth!

Doctor gags—Poke fun at doctors, especially their fees and occasional seeming lack of concern for the patient's discomfort:

> The doctor told me confidentially that your medical
> report looks terrible!
> . . . he dropped it in his spaghetti in the hospital
> cafeteria and it's a real mess!

ANNIVERSARY

Anniversary cards run the gamut from the complimentary to the irreverent, which poke fun at marriage. Whatever themes are used, however, they should wish the recipients happiness on that day and in the year ahead. The message must never end on a down note.

Philosophy—These cards range from being slightly suggestive to kidding about marriage. They simply imply that, in spite of everything, there will always be life in a good marriage.

Happy Anniversary, and remember . . .
. . . you're not OVER THE HILL
    till you're OVER THE THRILL!

Wish/gag—Suitable for sending to almost anyone, these cards do not compliment the recipients or comment on the happiness of their marriage. Here's a simple (but funny) wish or gag:

On your wedding anniversary, there's been
a TERRIBLE MISTAKE! Your marriage license
was signed by the wrong official and you
two are not legally married!!
. . . please return all wedding gifts
and children!

Any major theme can be combined with a *sub-theme* used primarily to personalize the humor in the studio card and to narrow the area of interest. The following are some typical sub-themes:

Business—Cards especially for workers joke about the boss or the economy, or the coffee breaks or questionable work habits of the crew:

Happy Birthday from one member
    of the rat race . . .
        . . . to another.

Sports/athletics—Gags using the most popular sports (golf, tennis, bowling, football, etc.):

Hey, Sport . . . how's it goin'?
Hey, Sport . . . how's it goin'?
. . . you've just received the world's first
greeting card instant replay!

The combinations are limitless. Make a list of the occasions, themes, sub-themes and humor formulas to keep near your typewriter for easy reference whenever you're looking for new ideas for humorous or studio cards.

꒜꒳꒘ CHAPTER 10

Cards for Children

CHILDREN TODAY ARE smarter and more aware than at any other time in history, and their parents and grandparents know it. If you are going to write successful cards for children, *you* have to be smarter and more creative than ever. The days are long gone when you could write and sell a dozen variations of

> This little kitten
> Has come to say
> "Have a happy,
> Happy day!"

The average child watches more than 16,000 hours of television before finishing high school. Children begin much of their learning process with *Sesame Street, Captain Kangaroo, Walt Disney,* and *The Muppets.* They cut their entertainment teeth on the adventures of *Wonder Woman, The Incredible Hulk* and *Superman,* and on space fantasies such as the motion picture *Star Wars.* They are exposed to catchy television commercials, well-researched textbooks, an endless supply of comic books, and the best reading books that the major publishers can put out. Today there is simply no excitement in a greeting card with "This little kitten . . ." type of writing. A child receiving such a card will simply open it, check to find any money enclosed, see who signed it, and then toss it aside and pick up his Amazing Spiderman superviewer.

To appeal to these very bright, aware, modern young people you must offer them strong ideas that are well-written in modern-sounding language and have attractive designs. And then, when possible, add "something extra."

Start by looking at the market you want to reach. Most card companies divide the juvenile market by age groups:

BABY—age 1 or under. Obviously, these cards are being sent to adults—the parent or parents of the infant, but the wording is usually directed toward the baby; the message is definitely sender-to-parent. An example:

> IT'S YOUR FIRST EASTER, BABY!
> Springtime is made
>   for everything lovely,
>   for everything new . . .
>   for bright, baby buttercups,
>   tulip buds, bluebirds . . .
>   and YOU!
> Hope your First Easter is very happy!

Note that there is purposely no direct mention of Mother, Dad or Parents, because it's possible that this is a one-parent baby, and any reference to "proud parents" would limit the sale.

PRE-SCHOOL—ages 2-4. Now you're dealing with children who can talk and walk and play; their vocabularies and interests grow almost daily. These children are the most creative of all. They are beginning friendships with other children and close relationships with adults.

Cards for pre-schoolers are selected and bought mostly by adults—relatives and friends of the family. The adults may be purchasing the card for children to send to children (as in the case of birthday parties, etc.), or for themselves to send. They realize that the pre-schooler receiving the card is not yet a reader and is still lacking the dexterity needed to handle "things to do" gimmicks. So the main emphasis is on the subject matter of the design (animals, trains, planes, boys, girls) and the message. The message should convey the wish for the occasion, deliver a compliment, or express a feeling (love and kisses, for example). An adult will read the card to the recipient, so there should be "sound effects" in the language chosen. Here's a typical pre-school card:

> (with an animated puppy design)
> HAPPY VALENTINE'S DAY!
> What's this coming in your mail
> With big, brown eyes and a waggly tail?
> Why, it's Pete the Puppy on his way
> To tell you HI on Valentine's Day!

Notice the possibilities for voice inflection on the part of the adult reading the card aloud? It's much more exciting for the child *and* adult than "this little puppy has come to say . . ."

SCHOOL AGE—EARLY GRADES—ages 5-7. Here you have the kindergarten to second-grade group—the youngsters who suddenly come into contact with classrooms full of contemporaries and adult figures (teachers) they haven't met before. They learn to read, write, and do arithmetic; they are creative, but in more structured ways (crafts, puzzles, games, sports) than pre-schoolers. Their social activities increase and social contacts are a more important part of their lives than ever before. Birthdays and holidays become more than just a chance for the child to be king or queen for a day. Interests are beginning to form and talents to take shape; the child is under increasing pressure to perform—and perform well. He takes delight in even the smallest accomplishment, because he knows it will mean some form of praise, a "reward" he has learned to seek.

Greeting cards sent to this age group are still primarily selected by adults, sometimes with the child sender present, sometimes without. Both adult and the youthful card senders should be aware of the importance of not "insulting" the recipient by talking down to him. Children this age like to be thought of as older than they are, but never, never younger. The design and language of the cards they are offered must reflect this. Consequently, the language begins to sound older:

SOME THANKSGIVING FUN FOR YOU
This maze may look tricky,
But you're very smart
So you won't have much trouble
In making a start . . .
Just keep your eyes open
Watch out for each clue
And in no time at all
You'll be all the way through!
HAPPY THANKSGIVING

SCHOOL AGE—MIDDLE GRADES—ages 8-11. These are third through sixth graders. School and school-related activities are a very important part of their daily lives, and they are busily pursuing specific interests (such as scouting, sports, science, art, music). Many are already earning small sums of money (paper routes, yard work, odd jobs, some baby-sitting). They begin to spend money by themselves and choose their friends. They may be involved in church activities, sports teams, slumber parties, and countless other group activities. Their need for recognition, praise, and love becomes greater, and they want it from contemporaries as well as parents and family.

Cards for this age group may be purchased by a variety of people, ranging from parents or adult relatives to contemporaries. Children are especially "choosy" about the cards they send, and because humor is so important at this age, they often try for a laugh with their greeting. At the younger end of the 8-11 scale, it may read like this:

> There are three things on your birthday
> that you just can't do without . . .
>   1. Making a wish
>   2. Taking a breath
>   3. Blowing your candles out

At the "older" end of the spectrum, the humor approaches that found in humorous and studio cards:

> (design: mouse with large swiss cheese, holes in it)
> Know why you're getting this "cheesy"
>   birthday card?
> . . . 'cause you're wished a "hole" lot of fun today!

> or

> Inside this birthday card you'll find
>   the complete tale of Peter Rabbit . . .
>   . . . (cottontail attachment)
>   HAPPY BIRTHDAY

PRE-TEENS—ages 11-13. This is a difficult age for card writers (as well as parents) to handle, because these young people are in various stages of leaving childhood behind. Their contemporaries are already sending them studio and humorous and Soft Touch cards, but the adults in their lives, who still send most of the cards they receive, are not quite ready to admit them to full-fledged teen-age status. Thus, pre-teen cards are still considered in the juvenile category, and the language in them is basically young adult—enthusiastic, upbeat, sometimes humorous, and tricky. The sentiments may run anywhere from:

> To be specific . . .
> . . . you're TERRIFIC!

to a funny approach:

> Guess what you get when you cross
> an ELEPHANT with a BIRTHDAY GREETING?
> . . . a card you'll never forget!

TEEN-AGERS—ages 14-18. This is another difficult age to write for, because there is such a great difference between the taste and maturity of a 14- and 18-year-old. Most card companies, therefore, subdivide their teen line into "early teen" (ages 14-15) and "late teen" (ages 16-18) and vary the language somewhat for the two groups.

While some of these cards are sent teen-to-teen, most are sent adult-to-teen. The adults realize that these young people have moved on from childhood and try to address them in a grown-up way. The card designs usually take care of identifying the recipient as a teen boy or girl, and the copy is either general and adult, or it attempts to talk the teen-ager's language. The latter is risky because the "in" vocabulary changes with the regularity of an armed forces secret code.

An example of the "young adult" approach:

> Happy Birthday! Hope the day couldn't be
> more to your liking . . .
> . . . even if you ordered it yourself!

An example of trying to "talk teen":

> A wild-and-crazy birthday Hi . . .
> . . . for a wild-and-crazy kind of guy!

There's danger in the latter because the word "wild" may be complimentary when you write it, but uncomplimentary by the time the card is published.

IDEAS

With your markets well in mind, you are ready to start writing children's cards. One of the best places to start is with "idea cards"—cards with "something extra," based on children's love of activity, movement, change and surprise. When you add something for the recipient to do (games, puzzles, stories, etc.), you make the card more than just a signature on a bright piece of paper: It becomes a little gift, too. There are several areas to explore here.

Things to do and make. There is practically no limit to what you can do with paper: with a little imagination, any greeting card can be the start of some fun activity for the recipient. Think in terms of punch-outs and cut-outs, paper dolls, a house with furniture, a farm with animals, a circus with animals and performers, a ranch with cowboys and horses, an air show with planes and pilots, outer space with orbiting space ships. Or take a slightly different approach—a paper crown to make; a disguise of eyes, nose, beard, and glasses to put on the face; little clothes and faces for Easter eggs; Valentines to make; postcards to make; Christmas decorations to make. Another approach—magic tricks, recipes, flower seeds and instructions for growing, a string with explanations of tricks with it, a bird-identifier chart (cut out and paste on bird picture in a spot when you see it), a sewing card with holes that make a design and yarn provided.

Games and puzzles. The challenge here is to think of something fresh enough to be new, simple enough to be mastered; inexpensive enough to be profitable, and small enough to fit into a greeting card. Try variations of mazes, hidden items in drawings, a plastic roll-the-ball-into-the-holes attachment, guessing games, treasure hunts, variations of pin-the-tail-on-the-donkey, simplified chess or checkers, card games, sports games, war games, business games, and creative games. This field has endless possibilities suited to greeting cards, if you think creatively.

Stories. Many of the familiar classics ("A Visit from St. Nicholas," "The Three Bears," etc.) have appeared on cards and will continue to be used, but original stories are always welcome. The problem is twofold: to tell a story in about 300 words (twelve to sixteen pages) and to tie the story into an occasion. These are fun to write. Just be sure your story fits the occasion and sending situation.

Novelties. These cards must offer something unexpected— a new riddle, a card with moving parts—mechanics that make a ghost pop up, or a device that makes a rocking horse move; a lion with a mouth that opens wide; a section of the artwork that disappears. A good place to find these novelties is in advertising gimmicks that come in your junk mail.

Instead of throwing them away, adapt and improve them for card ideas.

In using any of these ways to enhance the idea of the card and make it attractive to both the adult buyer and the recipient, never lose sight of the fact that a card is sent for a reason. And that reason should be noted in the sentiment. Make your idea and verse reflect the occasion or the season. Don't write a sentiment that could be sent *any* time and tack a "Merry Christmas" on it to make it a Christmas card! Use a mask for Halloween (that's appropriate); use a story for a Christmas card that is truly a Christmas story; and if you use a horse tie-in for a Valentine, give the horse heart-shaped spots and make that important to the sentiment. And never forget that whatever you include in a card, you are still writing a *card*; it needs an idea, a me-to-you message, proper greeting card form, and it needs to be sendable.

You can't go wrong in a juvenile card if you pay the recipient a compliment. So, when you are writing the sentiment to go with your "idea card," try to mention the recipient (favorably), the occasion, and the novelty. Here's an example:

> For You, Granddaughter
> Some jewelry for dress-up fun
> Bet you'll look like a princess
> (And a mighty sweet one, too)
> When you wear the jewelry, Honey,
> In this birthday card for you!
> HAPPY BIRTHDAY and HAVE FUN

When you're writing "activity" cards, try to incorporate the instructions into your sentiment. Children (and their parents) have a poor track record for reading printed instructions next to a diagram. It's your job in writing the message to instruct as well as pay a compliment and make a wish. Here's one way to do it:

FOR A FINE BOY'S BIRTHDAY
A Clown with a thousand funny faces
Hooray! It's your Birthday! And a fine boy like you
Is sure to have plenty of fun things to do . . .
But here's something extra—it's old FUNNY FACE
With eyes, nose and mouth you can put into place!
So, fix Funny's face silly ways, because gee . . .
Silly is really how clowns like to be!

You can compliment a young person further by not talking down to him. Use language that appeals to the age group for which you're writing and *not* an adult version of "children's talk" like this:

Hopin' your day's
'Zactly like you—
Nice 'n' fun
'N' really swell, too!

There are ways of using language that appeal especially to youngsters. The most successful approach is simply to talk to the youngster as if he or she were there in person—in a direct, conversational manner. Look:

A birthday, Honey?
Well, what do you know!
The bigger you get
The sweeter you grow!

Another good approach is the use of lively rhyme and meter.

Here's a birthday riddle for you!
You can't put it in your shoe
You can't ride it . . . you can't hide it
Now do you have a clue?
You can't climb it . . . you can't rhyme it
You can't feed it to a horse
Have you guessed yet what it is?
It's your BIRTHDAY, of course!

Don't be reluctant to upgrade the vocabulary you use in your juvenile cards. The vocabularies of children of the 1980's are many times greater than those of young people in the 1950's and 1960's, and there are very few words in everyday usage they won't understand. Ten years ago, most editors would have considered this sentiment "too adult-sounding," yet today it is a good seller:

For a wonderful boy
Take a little DARING
Stir some MISCHIEF in it
Add a dash of SUNSHINE
And GREAT FUN by the minute
Season well with SMARTNESS
LOVE 'N KINDNESS, too
And you have the perfect RECIPE for . . .
A WONDERFUL BOY like YOU!

Give the children a change to use *their* vocabulary, too. In your bag of tricks, keep in mind the "fill-in-the-blanks" approach which requires the recipient to do part of the writing. Here's an example which combines some upgraded vocabulary, tricky rhyming, and the "fill in" approach:

ALL ABOUT VALENTINE'S DAY
When someone says "Will you be mine?"
They want you for a _____
Some people think it's very smart
To give someone a candy _____
This might sound a little stupid
But the guy who flies around is _____
He flies as high as any sparrow
And shoots hearts with his bow and _____
And because YOU'RE nice, he's bringing this—
An extra hug and a great big _____

Keep in mind the basic honesty of children as you write cards for them to send and receive. Flattery that might be tolerated by adults will be spotted by children in a minute as corny or unbelievable. For example, few (if any) school-age children would be willing to send a card like this to a sibling:

Hi, Sister!
Hope your birthday turns out
Exactly like you—
Wonderful, perfect
And lots of fun, too

They know their sister may be lots of fun (at times), but they are around her often enough to know she's far from perfect. Forget the hyperbole and make your compliments simple and believable:

It's nice to have a sister like you
To wish a Happy Birthday to!

Finally, keep your sentiments as brief as possible. Remember that in the excitement of a birthday or holiday, a child goes through a lot of cards and gifts in a very short time and isn't interested in performing a reading assignment before playing with the presents or eating the goodies. State your message in a clear, clever way—then stop.

If you haven't tried writing juvenile cards before, you have a real treat in store for you. Once you get the hang of it, it's just plain fun. Many writers, in fact, prefer writing cards for children to all other kinds of greeting-card writing, perhaps because it gives them the chance to "be a kid" again. So, brush up on young people's youthful vocabulary, study your market, then have a go at it.

꧁ CHAPTER 11

Related Items

ALL MAJOR and most minor greeting card companies have a classification called "related merchandise," made up of items used to convey a message as well as serve as a gift in themselves. These were introduced by card companies only about 1970, so there is little backlog of written material and a great demand for new ideas from free lancers.

These related products are usually offshoots of a special kind of greeting card—the "something new" promotion, a series of greeting cards featuring either one style of artwork, a unifying character, or a special writing style (sometimes all three), displayed separately from the regular greeting cards. Many of today's familiar novelties started out as greeting-card promotions—Holly Hobbie, Ziggy, Betsey Clark, Strawberry Shortcake. Other promotions feature already-famous cartoon characters such as Peanuts, Mickey Mouse, Bugs Bunny, Tom and Jerry, and super-heroes such as Superman, Batman, Wonder Woman, and Popeye, plus the art and editorial style of well-known cartoonists such as Mort Walker (Beetle Bailey from the comic strips), the Berenstains (from *Good Housekeeping*) and Mordillo (European humor found mostly in books and posters).

As promotions grew into big business for the card companies, they began to look less and less like cards. Here are just a few of the industry's early classics:

> *Gag letters*—Letterheads that look like real business letters that are spoofs of existing companies, government agencies, magazines, etc.
>
> *Nutty announcements*—Cards done in a seemingly formal style to simulate invitations to parties, weddings, etc., but which actually parody such formality.
>
> *Musical greetings*—A combination of 45 rpm records and greetings, with the message recorded, often by a famous personality. Another variation of the musical approach is a series of music box greetings.
>
> *Dart boards*—Cards that open into humorous dart boards for various card-sending occasions. Each card has a real dart.
>
> *Sunbeam books*—Small, hardcover books that are substitute greeting cards and collectable items as well.
>
> *Silly-sculpts*—Three-dimensional characters that stand on desks or tables, and have messages on their bases ("For the World's Best Grandpa," "Thin may be in, but fat's where it's at!").

Notice how many of these promotion items go beyond the traditional paper item into a non-paper item. Many card companies have done a lot in producing such supplements to their card offerings. Today, most card firms have a variety of these, such as:

Ceramic plates—A message, usually serious, makes the plate a gift, a greeting, and a lasting keepsake. Classic approaches have been the use of "What is a Mother?" and "What is love?" on the plates.

Ceramic gift items—Vases, jewelry boxes, coffee mugs, balls, candle holders, and hundreds of figurines—all with short but powerful messages.

Picture frames—These carry wording on the frame itself as well as inside where the picture will ultimately go.

Other gift items—Ashtrays, clocks, banks, trivets, paper weights, collector eggs, salt and pepper shakers, etc. Most of these carry messages.

Buttons and badges—Especially popular around holidays to help promote the spirit of the occasion.

Christmas ornaments—A big business for card companies; nearly every successful ornament has written copy, ranging from the simple greeting to the more detailed message.

Back-to-school items—Notebooks, rulers, erasers, boxes, key rings, memo pads, stationery, pencils, pencil holders.

Paper products haven't been forgotten, either. Good sellers among the non-card paper items include:

Calendars—A big opportunity for writers because the varieties are large; there are always twelve to eighteen pages of copy, and copy is often required for each individual day as well as for the central "theme" of the calendar.

Party items—In addition to centerpieces, tablecovers, napkins, cups, there is a constant need for party-games booklets.

Posters—Idea-oriented posters that express some humorous or serious philosophy are closely related to spinoff items like *plaques* and *bumper stickers*.

Stationery—Including notepaper, scratch pads, post-cards, and lap-packs; nearly all of these novelty-line items require copy.

Invitations and announcements—Cellopacked items, such as party invitations, thank-you cards, birth announcements. There is fierce competition among the major publishers for this market . . . hence it is a good opportunity for the creative writer and idea person.

Books—Substitute greeting items that started as Sunbeam Books and are now a sizable line of books, on a variety of topics ranging from the very funny to the very serious.

The list of non-card items is long and continues to increase and change. Copy for these items may represent a large part of an editor's budget, so, to be a versatile greeting-card writer, you should be able to write this type of copy. Here are some tips for creating a greeting-card series—or promotion-related merchandise:

Promotions—Start with an idea. Think of a concept that will adapt itself naturally to several cards (anywhere from a dozen to fifty or more). Try some examples and don't do a whole line until you've sold an editor on the concept; you could end up wasting time and creative effort if an editor doesn't like it. Usually six to eight cards will convey your idea. For starters, make half of them birthday, the others friendship or no-occasion cards. Don't bother with minor captions, like Wedding, Anniversary, Baby Congratulations. Make your ideas fresh and new; rehashes of old approaches will get you nowhere. Don't go too far toward the unique or original, either. Aim at as wide an audience as you can. Be brief and timely. An example from the well-known Cheap Shots promotion (using old movie stills on the cover and funny punch lines inside) is the following, which portrays a woman surrounded by the Keystone Kops. It reads:

May the force be with you!

Following on the heels of *Star Wars*, it was timely; it was also sendable for birthday, illness, anniversary, baby congratulations, or nearly any occasion.

Keep the cards sendable, but be sure the copy ties in with the design idea. For example, a promotion that uses road signs as the design theme might show something like this:

CONSTRUCTION AREA AHEAD
(inside)   I really dig you!

This is fine. It's a good positive message and ties in well. Here's another one:

ONE WAY STREET
(inside)   They've named a street after
           our relationship

But the negative message here kills the sale. How many people would pay good money to slam a partner that way?

Avoid the esoteric. One writer submitted a promotion idea built around signal flags used by boaters. It was cleverly done, and the boating enthusiasts loved it, but there aren't enough of them to make a market.

Greeting Books—Remember when writing these books that ideas are as critical as the copy. Books are really substitute greeting cards. They should be good me-to-you messages for birthday, get-well, friendship, love, and sometimes seasons, so they are competing with cards for the customers' money and appreciation. If they are "just another card," they won't make it. But if you can give the book a special twist that makes it worth the 24-or-so pages, you will have a winner. The amount of copy isn't important. What is perhaps the best-selling Sunbeam book of all time had only seven words. The cover read: "When you're not around . . ." The last page read: "Nothing goes right." The rest of the book consisted of funny situations in which Ziggy found nothing but daily disasters which were portrayed in cartoon style. On the other hand, another good seller had several hundred words, answering the question, "What is a Mother?"

Writing greeting books isn't easy. Be sure to study what's on the market to get an idea of length, tone, and art possibilities.

Calendars—There's a certain kinship between calendars and books. Both require a good idea and a major investment in concept and writing time. Both can be very rewarding when you click.

There are many approaches to calendar-writing—serious (inspirational quotes, recipes, daily advice, religious messages), cute (dogs and cats with clever sayings, characters like Holly Hobbie uttering homilies), humorous (a calendar of special events for drinking toasts with each day a holiday or something worth celebrating). Before you develop the entire calendar, it's best to write a brief description of your concept and include the first two or three months of copy. Submit this much, and then, if the editor likes the idea, you can work out the rest. If not, you haven't wasted so much time.

Posters—These look deceptively easy. They can be easy, *if* you look at the idea and copy from the viewpoint of the *user* of the product. A poster is going to be a part of his or her décor—in the office, bedroom, recreation room, kitchen, or workshop. It should be appropriate to the user's personality, talent, work environment, philosophy, or general attitude. It may be funny or serious, but it must be suitable for daily viewing by the user and those around him or her. Probably the best-selling poster of all time (aside from certain cheesecake items) shows a harried cat, struggling to hold on to a bar. The copy reads:

Hang in there!

See the wide range of uses it has? It works perfectly in the office, at home, at school—wherever there is daily pressure and stress—and it offers good, positive advice. Another good seller mixes advice and philosophy:

Keep Smiling!
(it makes people wonder what
you're up to)

Closely related to posters are *plaques*. The copy may be similar, but is usually more personal and often more closely related to the work environment than posters (there's less space available in the average work area). Good, funny approaches have done very well. Examples:

You wanted it WHEN?!?!?!?

When I want YOUR opinion, I'll BEAT it out of you!

CREATIVE MINDS are seldom TIDY.

Please don't WAKE me till QUITTING time.

Serious quotes do well on both posters and plaques—favorites being Shakespeare, Thoreau, the Kennedys, and occasionally lines from popular songs or the cinema. One of the most popular serious quotes is:

Today is the first day of the rest of your life.

But many good-sellers have come from newly-written lines of philosophy—comments like these:

> When you have a friend . . . you have everything
> What you are is God's gift to you.
> What you make of yourself is your gift to God.
> Life is fragile . . . handle it with prayer.

3-D Products—Much of the copy used on these items is "light" philosophy similar in tone to plaques and posters. The main difference, however, is length. Three-dimensional products have limited space for copy, so the wording must be brief but meaty. From three to six words are ideal, and a dozen is maximum on items like figurines, vases, cups, trinket boxes, etc. Some examples of good copy:

> Love isn't love . . . unless it's shared
> Think of me often . . . with love
> The time to be happy is now
> Love is for always

When there is only a slight word tie-in between the copy and the three-dimensional item itself, you have added a "bonus" to the product, as in a bud vase with the line:

> Friends are the blossoms in the garden of life

or a trinket box with this thought:

> Memories are the smiles of tomorrow

The sentiments on three-dimensional products are usually implied rather than stated. Instead of giving a friend a plate that says, "Happiness is having you for a friend," customers seem to prefer the less direct statement, like "A good friend is forever." Remember, what you write for ceramic items must stand the test of time. They are meant for continual viewing and therefore must express thoughts that are pleasurable and meaningful for rereading, maybe for years and years.

Not all three-dimensional products, of course, are ceramic. Keychains are a case in point; the copy for these is usually humorous and ties in somewhat with the product's use. An example:

> When I finally figure out where it's at . . .
> somebody moves it!

Buttons and badges are usually sold in connection with established holidays—Christmas, New Year's, Valentine's Day, St. Patrick's Day, Halloween—and for the most part, the copy lines are humorous and meant to serve as icebreakers at parties, work, or school. They may be comic— "Kiss me . . . I'm Irish" or timely, like "Uppity Women Unite."

Stationery—These items—notes, scratch pads, postcards, and lap-packs—use copy that is closer to greeting cards in that the me-to-you message is stated or strongly implied. It may range from "P.S. I love you" and "Thinking of You," to humorous lines like, "I have good news and bad news!" and "Life ain't easy!" Paper pads may take a more personal approach, identifying the writer or his philosophy. Here are two examples:

> NOTES FROM A SENSUOUS WOMAN
>
> Someday my ship will come in . . .
> and with my luck, I'll be at the airport

Invitations and Announcements—For years there has been a creative "war" between publishers to see who can put out the best-selling "cellopack" line and writers with ideas benefit.

Think in terms of design-sentiment tie-ins—the cleverer, the better. These are the categories to write for:

> *Party invitations*—Birthday (adult, juvenile, teen), Cocktail Buffet, Dinner, Coffee, Swim, Slumber, Surprise, Beer, Showers (bridal, baby, general), and general all-purpose invitations for *any* kind of party.
>
> *Announcements*—Birth announcements for boy, girl, either, twins, and adopted. New home, new address, new apartment, and divorce announcements.
>
> *Thank you*—All-purpose thanks, also for shower gift, baby gift, wedding gift, thoughtfulness.

Don't submit serious or conventional material for these items. Editors have plenty of that; the market is for novelty ideas, preferably humorous/studio or very clever. Here are a few examples:

> Birth Announcement: We've HAD it! . . . and it's a boy!

> Invitation: COMING ATTRACTION
>   on _____ at _____
>   A Super Production
>   Starring _____
>   Featuring brunch, lunch, dinner, drinks, other
>   Directed by _____
>   RSVP _____
>
> Thank you: Danke
>   Merci
>   Gracias
>   (thanks in several other languages)
>   . . . I don't know how else to say it! Thanks!

Keep your material short; cards are small and the purchaser must have room to write a personal message if he wishes. Art plays a key role here, so leave the artist enough room to be clever by keeping your words to a minimum.

As you can see, these "related merchandise" items offer a variety of avenues for your writing talents. Don't limit yourself to writing only cards. As with writing cards, though, if you want to prepare other items it's important for you to research the marketplace first, see which companies manufacture what. Not every firm makes all these items. Since these other products often reflect trends and changes in art, humor, and events in the world, you must keep up and learn to anticipate such changes so that instead of being a follower, you become a leader and innovator of fresh, new, exciting ideas.

CHAPTER 12

How to Sell What You've Written

SELLING THE greeting cards you write is your goal, and you will be more likely to attain that goal if you are realistic in your approach. Although it isn't easy to become a successful free lancer in this field, it can be done if you're creative, and have a practical approach to selling and marketing what you write.

Set up a system. Record keeping, attention to detail, accuracy, and discipline are essentials for success. A typewriter is a must; submissions must be typed to look professional and be easy to read. Editors *do* judge material by appearance. You'll need a file box for index cards, with dividers to separate various stages of your greeting-card writing:

Ideas you think of or find and will develop when you have the time

New sentiments typed in the proper form and waiting to be sent

Copies of submitted batches that have been sent to companies, with notations on each as to when and where sent

Sales of sentiments, with notations on each as to when purchased, by whom, and for what amount

As the file grows, you will need to expand each section into separate files. You may even want to make subdividers. For your Ideas and New Sentiments section, you may want subdividers for Anniversary, Birthday, Christmas, Valentine's Day, etc. Also, for your copies of messages submitted, you may want subdividers for each company.

You'll also need plenty of 3 x 5 cards or slips of paper, the accepted size for free-lance submissions. You may want to cut typing paper into 3 x 5 pieces or buy 3 x 5 paper pads, since lightweight paper is easier to fit into a typewriter with carbon and second sheet, and less expensive to mail. You can also cut 3 x 5 carbon-paper slips from standard-size sheets of carbon.

How to submit material. When each sentiment is finished to your satisfaction, file it by category until you have enough sentiments in a category—10 or 12—to submit in a batch to an editor. You either may start sending them or write first to greeting card publishers for their "needs list" or "market letter." *Always* enclose a stamped, self-addressed envelope with your request for such a list or letter. Send your request to the editor by name, if you know it, or simply to Studio Editor, Humorous Editor, Conventional Editor, or Juvenile Editor. These needs lists or market letters tell you what an editor needs *most* at the time. You'll have a better chance of selling *that* kind of material to him *now*. Send a batch of sentiments *promptly* (editors have deadlines).

Type one sentiment on each 3 x 5 card or slip. In the upper left corner of each one, type an identifying caption (Birthday, Christmas, Illness, etc.) to help the editor when reading and you when filing. Type captions and tag lines in capital letters and leave space between them and the sentiment. If you are typing a sentiment that is partly on the cover of the card and partly inside (humorous, studio, etc.), leave a space between the cover copy and the inside copy.

Sympathy
IN DEEPEST SYMPATHY
May it help to know
that others care
and understand.

Birthday
This birthday card for you
has been rated X

. . . because you're Xtra
special!
HAPPY DAY!

Type neatly and correctly. If, after sending a sentiment to several companies, it has not been sold and becomes stained, wrinkled, or dog-eared—retype it. The way you present your material affects your sales.

On the back of each sentiment ORIGINAL, upper right or left, put your name and address and an identification number for that specific sentiment. You may simply number each card consecutively, starting with 1 and continuing through the batch. Keep a tally sheet by your desk to jot down the last number you use so you'll know what number to start with on the next batch—or devise a system of your own, but be sure to use a different number on each sentiment (and identical number on the matching carbon). What identifying system you use is not important as long as you use one.

Submit only ten or twelve, all of the same category, in each batch—humorous, conventional—and don't mix types. Don't use paper clips—they leave indentations in paper and necessitate constant retyping to keep your submissions neat.

On the back of your carbon of each sentiment, put the identification number in the upper left or right corner. Below that, put the name of the company to whom you sent it and the date sent. File the carbons in your "batches that have been mailed." If the card is rejected, write the date it's returned. If the card is accepted, write the date and the amount for which it is to be purchased; when the check arrives, mark the date on your carbon and add "paid." Here's a sample:

```
1042

Company A   4/5/8-      4/30/8-
Company B   5/5/8-      5/29/8-
Company C   6/4/8-      6/25/8- buy for $25
7/15/8- paid $25
```

Sometimes when a company purchases a card, you may be asked to sign a release and return it. This formality is for their records, as the check itself usually has a release on it, too, showing that you warrant the material you are submitting is original and that you are offering it for sale to the company. File sold cards in the "sentiments purchased" section of your file and rejected cards back in the "waiting to be sent" section. Don't forget to look over a rejected idea first—maybe you can rewrite it and improve it before you send it out again.

Type one envelope to the company, stamp it, and put your return address on it. Type one envelope to yourself, stamp it, and fold it in half. Insert the folded envelope fold *down* (so a letter opener won't slit it in two when the outer envelope is opened) and slip it behind your batch of cards in the envelope to the company. Don't include a cover letter. Cover letters are almost always considered the mark of an amateur. The deadliest thing of all is to send a letter that begins, "My friends all love the things I write so much that they just insisted I send them to you . . ." Write a letter to the editor only in reply to personal comments or questions to you.

It may take from two weeks to two months to hear from an editor, but waiting time varies greatly. The volume of the mail received from free lancers is always heavy, and judging material takes time. Use your waiting time to write more material. After six to eight weeks, send a note asking briefly and politely about your material.

Never send the same sentiment to more than one company at the same time. If a sentiment is rejected, you can send it to another company, and then the next (noting the company's name, new date sent, etc., in your records).

Accept rejections. Don't become too attached to your work. Though it may feel a part of you, keep your perspective; the rejection of *it* is not a rejection of *you.* Even the best professionals don't sell everything they write.

Don't try to judge your own material. Most writers tend to overvalue their work and are then disappointed when that judgment isn't shared by an editor.

Here are just a few of the reasons your material may be rejected: Perhaps your sentiment isn't a card—it lacks one of the necessary ingredients. Perhaps the card you suggest is too costly to make. Perhaps it isn't suitable for that company's audience or market, or it simply isn't that company's type of card. They may publish only seasonal or studio cards, for example, and your card is a juvenile or conventional. Maybe something about your message doesn't appeal to that editor (everyone has personal preferences, prejudices). Try it else-where and it may seem exactly right to *that* editor. A com-pany may be overstocked with age-angle cards or "daughter" cards at that time and can't use any more for a while. Many free-lance budgets are limited to purchases that can be used immediately, so if you send a Christmas card at the Easter scheduling season, it won't sell no matter how good it is. Their sales experience may indicate that your card will be a poor seller. This is something you couldn't possibly know when you submitted it. There are some other reasons your card may not be purchased. In any case, you can be certain that editors have sound business (not personal) reasons for turning down material.

Writers' block. All writers have periods when they have trouble writing. The best way to conquer it is to keep writing. Set a time to start every day and stick with it for a set number of hours daily. Don't wait to be "inspired"; whether you feel like writing or not, WRITE! Take magazines, books, clip-pings, ideas you've jotted down, notes from research, greet-ing cards you admire—anything you can find to stimulate your thinking. Pick a phrase from a book of axioms, choose a word from a dictionary, take an expression from memory, a television show, a line from a song, a slogan in an ad—and see how many ideas you can generate. If you bombard your mind with ideas and discipline it to follow through, you simply have to produce cards. Once you establish control over the situation, you can repeat it with success day after day. Self-discipline is a big part of free lancing, and often the part that spells the difference between success and failure.

Writing greeting cards should be fun as well as work. Like any occupation, writing needs practice and enthusiasm. So keep studying the market, keep writing, and, as your messages sell, your new sentiment file will grow and your satisfaction will increase. You will find yourself successful in the delightful and rewarding world of greeting cards.

THE GREETING CARD MARKET

What follows is a representative listing of greeting card companies that are currently looking for material; however, since needs vary, publishers move, and editors come and go, this market list may become dated. It's a good idea, therefore, to consult the greeting card market lists in *The Writer Magazine* and *The Writer's Handbook*, which are regularly brought up to date. There you will find the names of current editors and their specific requirements, plus useful tips on what they *don't* need. Another good source of information is a pamphlet including a list of publishers of greeting cards and related items. This is available on request (send a stamped, self-addressed envelope) from:

National Association of Greeting Card Publishers
600 Pennsylvania Ave., S. E., Suite 300
Washington, DC 20003

Amberley Greeting Card Company—P.O. Box 37902, Cincinnati, OH 45222. Ned Stern, Ed. Humorous studio greeting card ideas, for birthday, illness, friendship, congratulations; miss you, thank you, retirement, apology, goodbye. Risqué and non-risqué humor. No seasonal cards. Motto ideas and bumper stickers. Pays $25. Buys all rights.

American Greetings Corporation—10500 American Rd., Cleveland, OH 44144. Carl Goeller, Edit. Director. Always looking for good, fresh ideas for promotions, new products. Pays top rates for outstanding studio and humorous gags, juvenile card ideas. Buys some conventional material, but it must be well-written and up-to-date. Open to good ideas for related products—posters, calendars, plaques, and dimensional products.

Barker Greeting Card Co. (Division of *Rust Craft Cards, Inc.*) — Rust Craft Park, Dedham, MA 02026. Bill Bridgeman, Humor Director. Ideas for studio and humorous greeting cards, everyday and seasonal. Special interest in studio ideas using attachments and mechanicals. Pays from $25. Send self-addressed, stamped envelope for Market Letter.

D. Forer & Company, Inc. — 511 E. 72nd St., New York, NY 10021. Ideas and designs for whimsical everyday and Christmas lines. Pays from $20 per idea, on acceptance.

Fran Mar Greeting Cards, Ltd. — Box 1057, Mt. Vernon, NY 10550. Stationery and pad concepts. Party invitations. Thank you notes. Pays $25 per idea, within 30 days of acceptance.

Fravessi-Lamont, Inc. — 11 Edison Pl., Springfield, NJ 07081. Address Editor. Short verse, mostly humorous or sentimental; studio cards with witty prose. No Christmas material. Pays varying rates, on acceptance.

Gallant Greetings Corporation—2654 W. Medill Ave., Chicago, IL 60647. Ideas for humorous and serious greeting cards. Pays $30 per idea, in 45 days.

Gibson Greeting Cards, Inc.—2100 Section Rd., Cincinnati, OH 45237. Address Editorial Dept. Studio, humorous, and general material. Pays $50 for humor (must be short and punchy); $50 for studio; $3 per line for rhymed verse; $20 for "cutes" or prose. Especially interested in good "page 2" material appropriate for a season, occasion, or relationship, tied in with direct message for "page 3." Birthday (including all family birthdays), illness, cheer, wedding anniversary, sympathy for everyday line; general and family captions for all seasons. Juveniles. Pays following acceptance.

Hallmark Cards, Inc. — 25th and McGee, Kansas City, MO 64141. *Contemporary (Studio) Cards;* standard payment, $60 per idea. No artwork. Send to Contemporary Free-Lance Editor. *Humorous-Illustrated Cards;* standard payment, $66. No artwork. Humorous, clever ideas, softer humor and rebus writing. Send to Humorous-Illustrated Free-Lance Editor. *Hallmark Editions;* no free-lance material. *Hallmark General Verse and Prose;* no free-lance material.

Alfred Mainzer, Inc. — 27-08 40th Ave., Long Island City, NY 11101. Arwed H. Baenisch, Art Director. Everyday, Christmas, Mother's Day, Father's Day, Valentine's Day, Easter verses. Pays varying rates.

Mark I — 1733 W. Irving Park Rd., Chicago, IL 60613. Sensitivity verses; ideas for studio, everyday and seasonal cards. Pays from $35. Address Alex H. Cohen.

Mister B Greeting Card Co. — 3305 N. W. 37th St., Miami, FL 33142. Harry W. Gee, Ed. Humorous, risqué or novelty ideas, and serious, conventional or sentimental material, no more than 4 lines: Anniversary, Birthday, Get Well, Friendship, Mother's Day, Valentine's Day, Christmas, Jewish, and Special Captions. Pays varying rates. Replies in 4 to 6 weeks. Pays on selection of captions. Illustrations optional.

Norcross, Inc. — 950 Airport Rd., West Chester, PA 19380. Address Nancy Lee Fuller. Everyday and seasonal verse. Studio and humorous ideas. Pays from $20.

Paramount Line—Box 678, Pawtucket, RI 02862. Bernice Gourse, Ed. Humorous, sensitivity, prose and verse card ideas, casual approach preferred. Pays varying rates, on acceptance.

Red Farm Studios — 334 Pleasant St., Pawtucket, RI 02860. Informal cards, for birthdays, get-wells, anniversaries, friendship, new baby, retirement, new home, Christmas, and sympathy. No studio humor. Pays varying rates.

Reed Starline Card Co.—3331 Sunset Blvd., Los Angeles, CA 90026. Reed Stevens, Ed. Short, humorous studio card copy, conversational in tone, for sophisticated adults; no verse or jingles. Everyday copy, for birthday, friendship, get well, anniversary, thank you, travel, congratulations. Submit material for fall holidays in February; for Valentine's Day and St. Patrick's Day in May; and for Easter, Mother's Day, Father's Day in September. Pays $40 per idea, on acceptance.

Rust Craft Greeting Card, Inc. — Rust Craft Park, Dedham, MA 02026. Address Editorial Director; humorous material to Humor Director. Greeting cards for birthday, illness, friendship, etc., both humorous and general. Pays from $15 for informal and cute cards with strong illustration possibilities; from $10 for imaginative, sentimental prose; from $25 for juvenile and humorous, on acceptance.

Sangamon Company — Rt. 48 West, Taylorville, IL 62568. Andrea Koonce, Ed. Four- to eight-line rhyme or prose verse, traditional and humorous, for birthday, friendship, new baby, Christmas, etc. Ideas for contemporary cards. Pays $1.50 per line, on acceptance.

Vagabond Creations — 2560 Lance Dr., Dayton, OH 45409. George F. Stanley, Jr., Ed. Specialty cards, graphics on cover and inside punch line: birthday, everyday, Valentine, Christmas, and graduation. Mildly risqué humor with *double entendre* acceptable. Ideas for buttons. Pays $15, on acceptance.

Warner Press Publishers — Anderson, IN 46011. Dorothy Smith, Verse Ed. Prose sensitivity and verse card ideas, religious themes. Submit Christmas material in November, other material in September. Pays $1 a line, on acceptance.